TITUS

Life in the Church
Revised Edition

TITUS

Life in the Church
Revised Edition

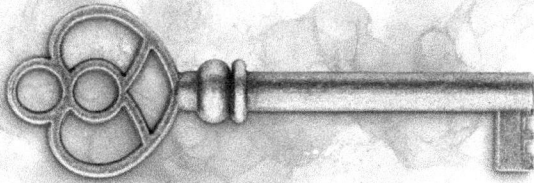

A Devotional Commentary

By

Bradley W. Maston

TRUE GRACE BOOKS

Titus: Life in the Church, A Devotional Commentary, Revised Edition

Copyright © 2024 by Bradley W. Maston

True Grace Books, *Tacoma, WA*

Published by True Grace Books LLC

Titus: Life in the Church, A Devotional Commentary / Written by Bradley W. Maston / Forward by E Dane Rogers.

Library of Congress Control Number: 2024903574

ISBN: 978-1-7327779-6-5 (Paperback) — 978-1-7327779-7-2 (Kindle)

1. Scripture.   2. Commentary.   3. Bible Study   4. Bible

Cover design by E Dane Rogers
Graphics by Canva, licensed use

Printed in the United States of America

2   4   6   8   10   9   7   5   3   1

TABLE OF CONTENTS

ACKNOWLEDGMENTS

Upon the second edition of this practical little commentary, my heart is filled with gratitude. To my parents, Bill and Karen Maston, who taught me what Christlike leadership is all about. To Vern Peterman who gave me the tools needed to dig into Scripture more deeply to find out what God's word truly says. To my friends Kevin Burch, Peter Adair, Jeff Maston and Bryan Park who first gave occasion to write this study for our meetings in a little coffee shop in Denver, Colorado. Then the army of people from Fort Collins Bible Church who read and improved this text for its first publication. Jackie Resseguie, Ruth Daley, Ellen Bjorhus, and others provided great insights in making this little book readable.

There are many others to thank for putting forth a second edition of this volume. Thanks to Dane Rogers for his patience in editing and typesetting, as well as providing the motivation to see the task completed. To Erin Pace, for the hours of editing and excellent edits and insightful recommendations. It is a simple reality that there would be no book were it not for the sacrificial works of others who love the Lord and long to serve Him.

Finally, I must acknowledge the Lord Jesus Christ, who by His Life, offers us the same. By His death, He offers the forgiveness of Sin, and by His resurrection, He gives those who believe the ability to walk in newness of life. May we no longer ask the foolish questions about what works or what does not, but ask the question, "What does the Lord want for His Church?"

FOREWORD

It's with the greatest joy that I add my brief foreword to this second edition of Dr. Bradley Maston's devotional commentary on Titus. In only a few dozen pages, Dr. Maston brings to life one of the Paul's shortest letters and helps the reader to engage it meaningfully and confidently. While many commentaries are much lengthier, meant to be read as a running dialogue with the reader, this commentary goes to great length to drive the reader into the text of Scripture. In that way, this is a companion, not a replacement for reading and understanding the book of Titus.

Maston explains many cultural, linguistic, lexicographic, and theological concepts in a clear, concise, cohesive, and comprehensible style. In these brief textual explanations, Maston artfully blends academic capability and genuine care for the reader. Maston will not try to impress with verboseness, but with simple clarity and precise interpretation, together with example applications that correspond with his careful exegesis.

The nature of this work makes it a perfect tool for personal or group Bible study. It is our hope in putting forward this volume that it will serve the body of Christ most generously for the glory of God. It has the potential to become a pocket classic.

May you, the reader, find this humble volume of genuine value, and may your study of the book of Titus bring you ever closer to our dear Savior and the amazing grace and eternal life into which we have entered through our common faith.

Grace and peace!

E Dane Rogers

INTRODUCTION TO THE BOOK OF TITUS

The Book of Titus

The Book of Titus is a letter from the Apostle Paul to a man named Titus who was a Gentile convert to Christianity (Gal 2:3). It was probably written around the same time as First and Second Timothy and shares a lot in common with those letters. All three letters were written to men that Paul had personally trained instructing them how to select elders and how to run new churches. Because of these similarities, the three books together are often called "The Pastoral Epistles."

The Island of Crete

Crete is the fourth largest island in the Mediterranean. The first time we read about Crete in the New Testament is Acts 2:11. People from Crete are mentioned amongst the many other Jews and God-fearers who had been in Jerusalem at the time of Pentecost. These citizens of Crete were present when the disciples spoke in tongues and Peter gave his great sermon leading more than 3,000 people to believe in Jesus Christ as their Savior. Likely, these people returned to Crete and did not have much of an idea how to live out this new faith. When Paul came through and preached the gospel, he left Titus to appoint elders at the churches, and oversee the development of the new churches there.

Prior to this time the Island of Crete had been conquered several times. It had been attacked, taken over, or assaulted by the Dorians early on, later the Greeks, the Persians, and the Egyptians. Crete was also racked with civil war and internal struggles that were almost insurmountable. Later the island became a part of the Roman Empire, but still maintained its identity as a vile place.

The People of Crete

The people of Crete were famous for being deceptive. During the years of oppression Cretans gained a reputation for shipbuilding, mercenary activity, and fraud. Records show these people praying to their gods to help lie and cheat others with greater skill. This is a culture that may hear the gospel and cheer for Judas, selling out his master for 30 silver coins.

1

There were also stories around this time of people that tried to cheat a Cretan. Inevitably, the character would find the situation backfired on them so that they were *still* cheated by the Cretan. It came to the point where it became a proverb: "You can't Cretanize a Cretan!" Cretans were so morally confused that they thought that the people who were cheating the system were the heroes. They would have called the pirates the hero, or the gangster and not the police, or the martyr.

This should call us to examine our own culture. God called Christians *out* of this culture. He called them to live in direct contrast to this culture that surrounded them. Just like the Cretan culture there is much of every culture that does not honor God, and God calls us to be separated from that in every way. What does that mean to us as Christians in this culture now? These days we try so hard to be "culturally sensitive," but we must always remember, as Christians, that we are not of this world!

Titus, The Recipient

With this understanding of the Cretans in mind we must consider the job that Titus was given. Titus was Paul's friend and spent a great deal of time in discipleship training. When Paul called Titus to minister to this group and this culture it may well have seemed impossible. It reveals much about the character of Titus. He must have been a "can do" guy. A fellow that is willing to take on a huge challenge. Above all, he must have been someone who trusted in the transformative power of Jesus Christ in the lives of people. Titus must have been well grounded in God's grace to receive such a task.

Paul, The Author

One may think that Paul wasn't a very good friend for sending Titus in on such a difficult task all alone! But Paul had good reason to believe that the gospel was sufficient for the people of Crete. Paul considered himself to be the worst of all sinners. He was a persecutor of the Church and breathed murderous threats against Christians, day and night (Acts 9:1–2). Paul had been a horrible person, a murderer with a heart filled with jealousy and hatred—yet God transformed him. The gospel changed Paul's life and he expected that it would do the same thing for the Cretans. Paul did not expect Titus to change them, nor did he expect them to change themselves. He expected God to change their hearts through the Holy Spirit. The Lord is still changing lives in this way, every day!

OUTLINE

I. Salutation (1:1–4)

II. Qualification of the Elders (1:5–9)

III. Characteristics of False Teachers (1:10–16)

IV. Godly Behavior for Different Groups (2:1–10)

    A. Older Men (2:1–2)

    B. Older Women (2:3)

    C. Younger Women (2:4–5)

    D. Younger men (2:6–8)

    E. Slaves (2:9–10)

V. Role of Grace in Promoting Godly Behavior (2:11–3:11)

    A. The educating power of grace (2:11–14)

    B. The gracious behavior (2:15–3:2)

    C. Grace as a motivation for godly living (3:3–8)

    D. Behavior inconsistent with grace (3:9–11)

VI. Final Instructions and Greetings (3:12–15)

---

[1] A. Duane Litfin, "Titus" in *The Bible Knowledge Commentary: New Testament*, eds. John F. Walvoord and Roy B. Zuck (David C Cook, 2018), 761.

TITUS 1:1–4

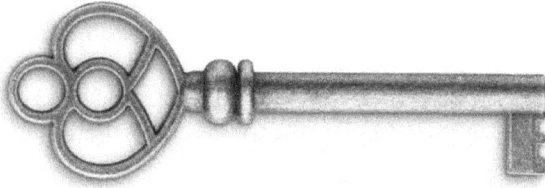

Salutations!

The outline calls this section the salutation or greeting. This greeting is one of the longest of all of Paul's greetings and it is packed with meaning. The primary focus of this greeting is to announce that Paul is a servant of God. It talks about God the Father and His character. Paul is very clear about who is in charge, and what we need to be concerned about.

Verse 1

*Paul, a **bond-servant** of God and an **apostle** of Jesus Christ, **for the faith** of those **chosen of God** and the **knowledge** of the truth which **is according to godliness**…*

Bond-Servant

Other translations use the word "slave" to translate this word. The word Paul uses here is *doulos*. It is the Greek word for slave. In the first century there were many slaves. By many estimates, there were more slaves than there were free people in the Roman Empire of this period. There were also multiple ways in which someone could become a slave or a bondservant. One could be born a slave or a bondservant. One could be sold into slavery by one's father, or husband. One could also become a slave by being too far in debt. At times people sold themselves into slavery to pay off debts.

In the Hebrew world we find many of the same regulations and rules for becoming a slave. If a person fulfilled their debt, or raised enough money he could buy himself out of slavery. We find in Scripture that each of us was "bought with a price" (1 Cor 6:20) and gain much of our identity, as Paul did, by Who bought us, and the price paid at the Cross.

4

The fact that Paul calls himself a slave shows his attitude towards God. He views himself as being bought and owned by the Lord, his will and being fully subjected to Christ. Just as a servant would look to the hand of his master, so Paul looked to the will of God to direct his steps and plans in this life. This leads naturally to consider the assignment which God gave Paul.

Apostle

The word "apostle" comes from the Greek word *apostolos* meaning: "a commissioned messenger." It was different from the normal word translated messenger (*angelos*) in that it was someone officially commissioned to complete a task and given the authority to complete that task. If a king sent a messenger, that messenger can only give the message, but an Apostle is given the authority to act in the name of the King to make it happen.

Paul is an Apostle of the second of two categories. In the first category of Apostles are the 12 Apostles that Jesus appointed during his ministry. Judas hanged himself and was replaced by Matthias in Acts 1:26. However, there was a second category of Apostle who had only to have beheld (seen with their own eyes) the risen Lord and have been commissioned by Him. The second category of Apostle was not inferior to the first, only different in type.

For the Faith

Paul makes it clear that his commissioning as an Apostle, as well as his servanthood to God has a purpose. It is for the faith of others that Paul has been called into the ministry. This is the purpose for his sufferings and his struggles. Comparing Paul's gift of apostleship with the other major passages on spiritual gifts in Romans 12, 1 Corinthians 12–14, Ephesians 4, and 1 Peter 4:7–11 reveals that this is the sole purpose of the spiritual gift—to edify and equip believers in the body of Christ. The same is true of the believer's service in the church today. There are any number of ways that we might serve the body, but the goal of that service is to build believers up into a mature faith in Christ and what the word of God reveals.

Chosen of God

The word for chosen of God is *eklektos*, or the elect of God. It comes from two words: *ek* meaning "out," and *lego* meaning "word" or "called." So, this is the "out-called." These are the ones who are called out by God. This biblical word has caused a great amount of discussion in the church, mostly because it is often defined in philosophical terms, rather than historically, culturally, and in the greater context of Scripture.

This word had an interesting use in the culture of the New Testament times. William Barclay observed about this concept:

> *F. J. A. Hort rightly points out that originally the word does not mean, as it is so often stated, a body of people who have been 'picked out' from the world. It has not in it that exclusive sense. It means a body of people who have been 'summoned out' of their homes to come and meet with God; and both in its original Greek and Hebrew usages, that sense was not exclusive but inclusive. The summons was not to any selected few; it was a summons from the State to every man to come and to shoulder his responsibilities; it was a summons from God to every man to come and listen to and to act on the word of God.*
>
> *In essence, therefore, the Church, the ekklesia, is a body of people, not so much assembling because they have been chosen to come together, but assembling because God has called them to Himself; not so much assembling to share their own thoughts and opinions but assembling to listen to the voice of God.*"[2]

Knowledge

The Greek word that Paul uses for "knowledge" here is *epignôsis*. This is different from the Greek word *oida*—which is knowledge by

---

[1]William Barclay, *A New Testament Wordbook* (New York: Harper & Brothers Publishers, 1960), 35.

perception—something learned by being told or read in a book. *Gnosis* means actual, practical knowledge. It is also focused on the highly involved relationship between the knowledge and the learner. This is the kind of knowledge that comes from being personally involved in the substance of what is learned. The word Paul uses here adds the prefix *epi*—which here functions to intensify the level of understanding. To illustrate, a person may have *oida* knowledge having read how to change oil in a car manual. That person would have *gnosko* knowledge after changing the oil himself. Not until that person had changed the oil in the car several times and really understood how the whole system worked would he have an *epignosko* type of understanding. This final level of understanding is what Paul reveals about the truth. As a believer studies the word of God we are growing in this level of knowledge—not just superficial hearsay—but real personal and functional knowledge of God and his plans and purposes for us.

According To

The word *kata*, in the Greek, could be translated "in complete accordance with." This is important in this passage and here it means that it is in full accordance with truth. This would be quite striking in the context of the Cretan culture, where lying, cheating, and stealing would have been admired. Biblically, truth has a moral component, this differs from our modern western viewpoint. The truth or falsehood of a particular claim does not have a particular moral charge in secular western thinking.

If the statement is made: "the chair is in the corner," then the chair is simply in the corner, or it is not. If the chair is in the corner, then the statement is true, and if not, the statement is false. However, what is revealed in the Bible is not just a set of cold facts, it has a moral purpose in revelation. The Bible reveals the truth of God, and anything that contradicts biblical revelation is not only "false" but leads to error and deception. Taking a stance that is ignorant of, or in contradiction to, the Bible is not just incorrect it leads to ungodliness, sin, and destruction.

Godliness

This is an interesting word. It is translated "godliness" but the word itself is *eusebeia*. It means "well directed reverence". The word "God" is

7

not in the Greek word at all. It really focuses upon the outward holiness of the believer. Remember that this focus on outward holiness comes only from the knowledge and faith in Jesus Christ. The godliness is the result of union with Christ, not a sign of it, nor is it proof, but it comes as a natural product of our union with Christ. This means that if a believer's life fails to have this quality, they need a better understanding of Jesus Christ and the life that He has given the believer by His work upon the cross.

Verse 2

...in the **hope** *of* **eternal life***, which God,* **who cannot lie,** **promised** *long ages ago...*

Hope

The concept of "hope", in English, it is often used in the sense of a desired outcome that is uncertain. One may say: "I hope it doesn't rain!" with the meaning that the speaker wishes that it wouldn't rain, though it may very well rain anyhow.

In the Bible, hope is a different concept. Hope is the anticipation of an assured outcome or result. Hope is not a matter of *maybe* but a matter of *certainty*. When Paul talks about "the hope of eternal life" in this verse, he means that eternal life given to believers is certain. This is a definite way of expressing the guarantee of eternal life. If there was any chance that we could lose this eternal life, by any means or way, this statement would not be true. This absolute assurance is meant to provide the believer with the powerful sustaining force (hope) that will bring the Christian through the trials, fears, and uncertainties of this life. The promise of salvation is meant to impact the practical day-to-day existence of the one whom Christ has saved.

Eternal Life

The word for "eternal" in this verse is *aionios*. It is a word that means without beginning or end. It is something of an eternal character. Something could last forever and still not be *aionios* – or eternal. A rock may have lasted from the moment of creation until the consummation of the earth, and yet it is not eternal because it has a beginning, an end, and is vulnerable to be affected or destroyed in the context of the passage of time. If something is eternal, it is something that is no longer affected by time as we know it. Eternality is something that uniquely relates to God who alone is eternal.

"Life" in this sentence translates the word *zoe*. *Zoe* does not usually indicate biological living (or breathing) but on the life in the spiritual sense of the word. So, we see that we have the hope (promise) of eternal life, meaning spiritual life that exists outside of time.

Who Cannot Lie

This statement is not found anywhere else in Paul's writing and certainly not in his introductions. Why would Paul take time to point out that God cannot lie? The culture of Crete admired liars. They looked up to the deceivers and thieves. The gods in Greek mythology would lie and cheat just as soon as tell the truth. Scripture is clear: God cannot lie. Any word that He says or promise that He makes can only be truth. In the Greek this phrase comes across "the cannot-lie God" as cannot lie is one word. When we read the promises of Scripture, we must always remember that God is the "cannot-lie God."

Promised

This was something God promised long, long ago. A promise from this "cannot-lie God" is trustworthy. We can lean on this promise forever; for God's promise is *always* good.

The phrase "long ages ago" could be more literally rendered "before times eternal." And reminds us of the fact that God had made His plan to send Jesus Christ "before the foundation of the world" (Eph 1:3–4; 2 Tim 1:9). Our salvation was planned out before the ages of earth began, we can count on God's sovereign plan to save us, keep us, and bring us into glory!

Verse 3

*...but at the **proper time** manifested, even His word, in the **proclamation** with which I was **entrusted** according to the **commandment** of God our **Savior**...*

Proper Time

This phrase could be translated "in His own timing." This word for time can refer to the right season, the perfect time, or a limited season of time. When the time was perfectly right for Jesus to come, God sent Him. Once again, the Salvation of God is in no way careless, flippant, or glib. It is not a plan that can fail, nor are there any "surprises" to God. It is a similar concept to what Paul taught in the book of Galatians:

"But when the fullness of the time had come, God sent forth His Son, born of a woman, born under the law, to redeem those who were under the law, that we might receive the adoption as sons" (Gal 4:4–5 NKJV).

God sent Jesus at exactly the right time, the right place, and to the right parents. Christ's coming was perfect in relationship to every prophetic expectation, as well as at the perfect time for the world to be able to spread that gospel to the very ends of the earth.

Proclamation

This word for "proclamation" ("preaching" in other translations) means "heralded as by a town crier". Before internet, television, and phone-trees this was one way important information got around. Imagine someone running through town crying out the good news of Jesus Christ. That is how Paul sees himself: preaching the gospel as a town crier out to share the good news. That is still the work of the church today – to spread the good news of the salvation that is available freely by God's grace in Christ alone. The task of preaching the gospel does not mean that believers must be "preachy" but rather that everyone is meant to publish this news in the broadest scope possible. Unbelievers need to hear the gospel message—that Jesus Christ, the Son of God, gave His life on the cross at Calvary to pay the penalty for man's sin. This message is only applied to the one who trusts in Jesus Christ alone for salvation. Christians must understand and be able to share this message for this is the gospel which has the power to save. As Paul wrote in the book of Romans, "For I am not ashamed of the gospel of Christ, for it is the power of God to salvation for everyone who believes, for the Jew first and also for the Greek" (Rom 1:16 NKJV).

Entrusted

Paul is clear that he did not invent this message, nor did he figure it out by his own intellect. This message was all given to him by God to proclaim to the nations. Paul is relaying God's messages, not inventing his own. He was entrusted with this message by God, and it is of the greatest importance. Paul is careful to preserve it and protect it. Throughout Acts and Paul's epistles he protects the doctrine of this teaching with his very life, not allowing anything to pervert it. The Church of God is also entrusted to keep this message, and its purity, not allowing people to destroy, or change it for any reason (Acts 20:29–30; 2 Tim 3:6–9, 12–13; 2 Pet 3:16).

Commandment

This proclamation is in full accordance with the commandment (and authority) of God. Once again, Paul makes it clear that the source of all of this is God. God is the source of our salvation, and the source of the Church. God is the source of the Scripture, as it is breathed of Him (2 Tim 3:16).

Savior

The phrase "God our savior" is not found outside of the Pastoral Epistles (1 & 2 Timothy and Titus). It is something that Paul chose to highlight in these books and not elsewhere.

In Roman times, when the emperor would come and visit a city or a town everyone would gather to watch him pass in parade. It was required that they would shout and chant "Savior, Savior." The Romans credited the emperor with saving the world. For Paul to say that God is the exclusive savior would be to imply that the emperor is not the savior. This doctrine would cause a lot of trouble for Roman patriots.

Verse 4

...to Titus, **my true child** *in a* **common faith: Grace and peace** *from* **God the Father** *and* **Christ Jesus our Savior.**

My True Child

Many commentators think that this referred to Paul being the one who led Titus to the Lord. Regardless of that possibility it is very well agreed that Titus was Paul's *protégé*. Paul discipled Titus, meaning he trained him up and taught him how to be a leader in the Lord. This concept of discipleship is sorely missing in the Church today. We see in Biblical history that the emphasis on discipleship was always important in the transmission of the faith. The teaching that comes from years studying the Word and walking with Christ is meant to be transmitted through the life-on-life process of disciple making. This is not just a transfer of information, but a process of transformation.

Common Faith

The word "common" here is from the same word that we often translate "fellowship." There are several important applications. First, faith is not something that exists only between the believer and God but is something that is shared and exists between all believers. The Bible teaches that believers are the Body of Christ—corporate identity is important. This is especially difficult to understand considering the individualism of western culture. It can be challenging for the western mind to subjugate individual identity to corporate identity, yet this is exactly what Scripture puts forth. Rather than the focus upon the specific things the individual thinks or believes, the focus of the believer should be to agree with everything the Bible reveals. There is no place for a unique faith, or private doctrine in the body of Christ—the Church is meant to be united by a common faith. This is the faith revealed in the Bible.

Additionally, a common faith is something to preserve and work towards. We often find heretics are identified by the things that they believe uniquely. We see these men lurking around the body looking for a chance to share their own "secret doctrine," or some point they differ with the faith of the local church or the pastor. In contrast to the *laissez-faire* attitude of the modern church the Scripture repeatedly commands the saints to be "speaking with one voice" (Rom 15:6), be of "the same mind" (1 Cor 1:10), and the reality that we should be attaining to "the unity of the faith" (Eph 4:13).

Grace and Peace

The common Gentile greeting at this time would be "Grace" and the Hebrew greeting would commonly be "peace". Amongst the Gentiles grace was an undeserved gift, or a gift that was not expected to be paid back. This was something that the Gentiles would *never* expect of their gods. Greek gods were worse than gumball machines. The devotee was expected to give to them, and they may or may not grant any requests. They would never be the first to give. But Paul opens his letter to Titus reminding him that God has been the one who has freely given to us, grace like an ocean or a waterfall to cover all our needs.

Through Christ's death on the cross we have been given peace. We have been given peace with ourselves because Christ has separated us from our old sin nature (Rom 6, Gal 2:20). We have been given peace with our fellow brothers and sisters in Christ because of the love and the peace that He pours into us. Most importantly, however, we have been given peace with God (Rom 5:1). While we were still enemies, Christ died for us and made peace between us and God possible (Rom 5:8).

This is how Paul chose to open his letter to Titus. It is his message to the people of Crete. Grace and Peace were two things that Cretan culture was lacking in great measure. There was no grace between people who were constantly trying to cheat each other, there could be no peace when neighbors can never be trusted. These things are the gift of God. Paul is not demanding that the Christians *make* grace or peace, but merely live in the grace and peace that God has given!

God the Father

Once again Paul chooses to highlight the fact that God is the Father, Our Father. God is the Father of fathers, and the origin of all fatherhood. Earthly fathers succeeded as they follow His model of fatherhood. They fail if they don't follow the model of God. He is our loving Father in Heaven. It is important in every human life to move beyond earthly fathers to enjoy the unique relationship of the child of God to the heavenly Father. This can be difficult both when a person's earthly father is an excellent and godly father-figure, or when the father-figure is particularly wanting. In both cases it takes an intentional choice to recognize the ultimate Fatherhood of God the Father in the life of the believer. This transfers all authority and final responsibility over to God and the care that He alone provides. When the believer regards God as his heavenly Father and treats Him as such God is most honored in the life of the believer.

Christ Jesus Our Savior

Paul credits this grace and peace as coming from "God the Father and Christ Jesus our Savior." God is referred to as "our savior" in verse 3 and Jesus is "our Savior" in verse 4. This is a reinforcement of the fact that Jesus is in every way God. He is united completely with God the Father and one with Him in the Holy Trinity.

TITUS 1:5–6

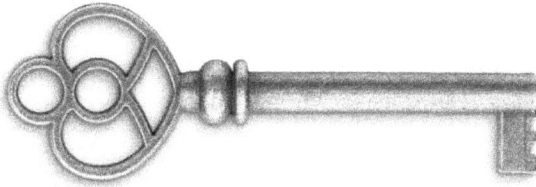

Qualifications of Elders

Having finished his greeting Paul gets right down to business giving qualifications for elders. The New Testament Church was ruled by appointed elders. The word "elders" appears multiple times to describe this position. Only one time (Eph 4:11) is the term "pastor" used in a sense that could be called a title. The rest of the time it is used as a verb. The office of elder is also described using the words "pastor" and "overseer" which describe the functions of the office. This is quite different from most churches today that may have an "elder board" but are really run by one controlling pastor or elder. This is not the biblical model. The biblical model found in Acts, Ephesians, 1 & 2 Timothy and Titus all confirm the idea that there are several elders working together to govern the Church.

Why is it important?

Why should a believer study these verses if they do not aspire to the office of elder? There are many reasons! The primary reason is that this list is not just a check list for elders, it is a picture of spiritual maturity. Spiritual maturity is the goal of the Christian life and how God is most glorified (Eph 4:13–16). Believers are to apply these principles. It shows us the kind of people that God is making, and the quality of life of a mature Christian. This is not an impossible list for the one abiding in Christ. It is the character of a person who is surrendered to Jesus and abiding in Him. Believing on Him, and studying and applying God's Word to reach maturity, he will exhibit these qualities by the grace of God. This is the good work that Christ is carrying on to completion in the believer!

When is all this happening?

All the verbs in this section are in the present tense. This list is not to be used as a law to forbid people the position of elder based on their sordid past. Many arguments have been made that a person cannot be an elder if he was divorced years ago. That is not found in the text here. These questions are about who this person is *now*, not who they were years ago. Furthermore, this list of character qualifications does not justify people chasing church leadership around with these lists disqualifying them at any imperfection. Established character is what is important before the Lord.

Verse 5

*For this reason I **left you** in Crete, that you would **set in order** what remains and **appoint elders** in **every city** as I directed you…*

Left You

Paul shows his confidence in Titus, reminding him that he left him here with a task. This task was entrusted to Titus alone which is saying a lot about the character of Titus, especially considering the nature of the island of Crete. It also made Titus Paul's special Apostolic delegate to appoint elders as an authority, not merely to make suggestions. This shows another theme about biblical eldership. While the qualification for eldership is the work of the Holy Spirit in the life of the believer (Acts 20:28), a person is appointed to eldership by others. In the Apostolic Era, it was the Apostles and their legates that made those first appointments. This means that a person does not recognize and appoint themselves as an elder, neither is it done by popular vote. This process means that a person must be edified, examined, and established in the faith before being appointed to a position of authority.

Set in Order

This is an aorist middle subjunctive. The "aorist" tense would suggest the idea that Titus was to "start setting in order" suggesting that getting the ball rolling in the right direction in each of these cities should set the churches there up for success. The "middle" voice suggests that Titus was supposed to do this himself. It gives the idea that responsibility for this task was solely on his shoulders. The "subjunctive", just as in English, is almost an imperative. Paul is saying "this is what you should do."

16

Appoint Elders

Titus is given the responsibility of appointing elders. Paul meant for Titus to seek out men of this certain character and appoint them to the office of elder over the rest of the people. This was a pattern that was intended to be continued by the elders, then choosing the next generations of elders. The idea being that the elders would have the wisdom to govern the Church body, as well as identify the people who would be able to lead after them. This system also gives younger appointees to the office the opportunity to learn and grow into the task of leadership. Whether lay-elders or vocational elders, there is an opportunity to lead the body from a place of community.

Every City

The fact that he was told to appoint elders (plural) in every city gives further support to the idea that the church body is meant to be led by several elders, not by any one person. At this point in the growth and development of the Church it is difficult to imagine each city having more than one church. It is most natural to think of there being a single church that would gather in each city. This verse finalizes what the Lord has in mind: multiple elders ruling each church body. The elders are selected according to the character standards in this book and in the epistle of Paul to Timothy. This method of Church governance has many advantages. It discourages Christian hero-worship. It also keeps the church family from being led astray because the leader got out of line. It keeps the pastor from suffering from lone leader syndrome and equips and empowers others to serve. However, it is important to note that this style of leadership is not the right way to govern the church owing to its strategic advantages. The Church should be run this way because it is how God's word declares that the churches must be administrated.

Verse 6

*...namely, if any **man is above reproach**, the **husband of one wife**, having **children who believe**, not accused of dissipation or rebellion.*

The Big List

This is the list of 17 qualifications that Paul puts forth for eldership of the local church. It is important to keep in mind that every believer is still growing, a sinful person in the hands of God. There will be no Christian without flaw and imperfection, thus we should not take this list to our church council for every minor flaw of an elder. This is not a law by which we should judge people. At the same time, it is not an impossible list and should not be viewed as lofty ideals that are completely unattainable.

Man above Reproach

This has also been translated "un-accused" or "blameless." It means that he is currently, right now, above any accusation that could be laid before him. This is the type of person that is not going to be accused or reproached by his fellow church members, or others outside of the Church.

Husband of One Wife

This phrase has given the Church a great deal of problems in the past. Some people want to interpret this to mean that he must only have been married to one wife, ever. This would mean that anyone who had ever had a divorce of any kind would be disqualified from eldership. This is one interpretation.

However, the present tense in this suggests more the quality of the man. It gives the sense of a "one-woman kind of guy." It doesn't say anything about what he was years ago, or what he had done in his youth. Rather, this addresses his current, lasting, character as one who is faithful to his wife. In the culture of Crete, it was considered perfectly legitimate to visit prostitutes, as with many pagan cultures around the world today. One quote from around this era was "We have our wives to bear our legitimate heirs, and our concubines for our own entertainment." Paul was seeking men who were living in contrast to their culture. He was not doubting the grace of God to forgive mistakes made years before, nor was he questioning God's ability to make a new and wonderful elder out of someone who had a sinful past.

Children Who Believe

There is already a bit of interpretation built into this translation of the verse. This verse could be translated "having children who believe" or possibly "having children who are faithful." The difference being that one focuses on the children as saved believers and the other focuses on their faithfulness and obedience to their parents. The second makes far more sense because it does not make sense for adults to be held responsible for the salvation of their children. Salvation occurs when a person chooses to place their faith in the sacrifice of Christ for their sin. It is entirely alien to Scripture to claim that one person is responsible for the decision of another to trust Christ.

The second option also makes more sense when compared to the next statement. The phrase "not accused of dissipation or rebellion" seems to imply their outward actions more than their faith in the Lord Jesus. It also places the focus for the elder: on his family. The man who is going to lead the church must be first be a leader of his family. Many men have destroyed their families in the name of "ministry", and I believe that God weeps over this tragedy. The first and primary ministry of any man is his family—obligations to the church are meant to follow that priority.

TITUS 1:7–9

Verse 7

*For the **overseer** must be **above reproach** as **God's** **steward**, **not self-willed**, **not quick-tempered**, **not addicted to wine**, **not pugnacious**, **not fond of sordid gain**...*

Overseer

This word "overseer" here has also been translated with the High-Church word "bishop." Both English words have the same meaning: one who watches over, protects, and leads. Many have tried to build doctrines that we are supposed to have "elders" and "overseers" from this and other passages. However, it does not take long to observe that Paul uses these words interchangeably (Acts 20:17, 28; 1 Pet 5:1–2). To Paul they were two words for the same office. It carries the idea of "the elders, who are also overseers" not two separate offices, but rather "Elder" is the office and "overseeing" is what that officer does.

Above Reproach

Again, the expectation for the elder is to be above reproach. This is not demanding perfection out of the elder, because no man could ever be found after Christ! However, it is reinforcing the high standard for this position of leadership. The idea, here as with the rest of this passage, is that there is not a current standing charge against him. This would be a distraction to both the elder and the body for him to have accusations leveled at him currently, with his character in question.

God's Steward

Stewardship is a very important concept in the Bible. God has worked throughout all time using stewardships, and each is very important. Even the idea of the "dispensations" would better be described as "stewardships." Every stewardship has a steward, a principle of stewardship, and a domain. As we look at past stewardships, we can look at Adam. Adam was given the stewardship over Eden. His stewardship was to care for it, multiply, and not to eat of the fruit of the knowledge of good and evil. The domain of his responsibility was over the earth.

Another biblical stewardship was the stewardship of human government. God, through the Noahic covenant, gave a stewardship to human governments that continues to this day, that they should maintain order. The major change was God's bestowal of authority to the government to take life from the murderer. The steward is human government, the domain the people under that government's rule, and the principle is that of law.

Understanding these stewardships clarifies a great deal. Moses had a stewardship, the domain was Israel, the principle was that of Law. It was then handed off into three separate stewardships, Prophets have had the stewardship of representing God to the people. The Levitical priesthood had the stewardship of representing the people to God, and the kings had the stewardship of ruling the national affairs of the people. This is why Christ's role as "prophet, priest and king" is so important during the Millennial Kingdom.

When it comes to governing the family every husband and father has a stewardship. The family is not his, but it is his to care for as God's chosen steward for the task. This is also how the church is to be ruled. Initially the church was ruled by Apostles, but when this gift expired, the stewardship was passed to elders. These elders are to act as stewards, entrusted with the management of the affairs of the body of Christ. Notice the stewards are the elders, the domain is the church, and the principle is the principle of grace.

Not Self-Willed

The Greek word translated "self-willed" here is *authadês*. It means "one who is pleased with himself and despises others, insolent, surly, the contrast of courteous or affable. A person who obstinately maintains his own opinion or asserts his own rights but is reckless of the rights, feelings, and interests of others."[3]

This is the type of person who is running his life in such a way that is thoughtful of himself before others, who is willing to act on his own behalf even though it is painful or inconvenient for others.

Not Quick-Tempered

The value of this quality is obvious. It would be a terrible thing for a church leader to be constantly working himself up into a fury over every tiny thing. It suggests a level-headedness. The word in Greek is related to the Greek word for wrath. It means that the mature Christian is not hot-headed. However, it does *not* mean that the mature Christian is weak or wimpy in any way. Not being quick-tempered does not mean someone who puts up with violations because of cowardice or inability to confront problems. The idea is that he is not easily provoked to fits of temper, one may say the biblically qualified elder has a "long-fuse."

Not Addicted to Wine

Even more so than today wine was a common drink of the people. However, just like today, there were those who would become addicted to it. The word in Greek for "not addicted to wine" is a compound word that would literally be translated 'not-next-to-wine.' Clearly the word picture is quite plain. The person who is always hanging out next to the alcohol source is clearly controlled by something other than the Lord, and this is unacceptable. It is, in fact, even a form of idolatry. Obviously, someone who is an alcoholic should not be chosen to lead God's people. However, it must be noted that this is by no means forbidding responsible drinking, that is not the purpose of this passage, and is totally foreign to the New Testament.

---

[3] Spiros Zodhiates, ed., *The Complete Word Study Dictionary: New Testament.* Revised, Accordance electronic edition, version 1.3 (Chattanooga, TN: AMG Publishers, 1993).

Not Pugnacious

Pug-a-whatty? Pugnacious is an uncommon word. It basically means one who is violent. Some have put it as a fighter, or a bruiser; that is, someone who is ready for violence. Paul also pairs these two qualities together in 1 Timothy. It may be the case that he is relating the two: that an addicted person is more likely to be a fighter. Either way this is not the type of person to lead the church. A person walking around looking for a fight, or an argument is not the type of person fit for eldership. Most can think of a person who seems always on the cusp of explosive anger. This is the kind of person for whom physical violence is the quiet background of their lives. This is not the character of Christ; this is an aggressive person.

Not Fond of Sordid Gain

This phrase indicates someone who is not greedy, or not motivated by dishonest gain. It is the type of person who will not cheat or lie or steal just to make some extra money for himself. This is an honest person who is not money motivated. Imagine if an elder of the church were accused of cheating on his taxes. It would destroy his testimony altogether to non-believers everywhere, and once again shows that something else (the love of money) is calling the shots, rather than the life of Christ within.

Verse 8

*...but **hospitable, loving what is good, sensible, just, devout, self-controlled**...*

Hospitable

Having finished a list of vices that should be avoided Paul moves onto traits that should be found in the believer. The word translated "hospitable" is a compound word combining the word for "love" and the word for "stranger." It has the idea of welcoming people into one's home. Peter extends this to say that hospitality should be offered "without grumbling" (1 Pet 4:9). This love for guests should be extended after they have left, not to grumble and complain about having had them.

Hospitality was especially important in the New Testament times because every inn or hotel during this time and in the greater Roman world would be a brothel. This means that even if the Christian could convince the owner to let him stay there without a prostitute his testimony would still be destroyed among the people of that community. In the modern world this is not such a great problem, thus it may be most hospitable to provide a traveling believer with a hotel room. The idea of having lives that are open to others is a concept more foreign in some cultures than others, yet this does not change the fact that hospitality is part of the Christian life.

Loving What is Good

This is another compound word that combines the Greek word for "love" with the Greek word for "good." This can be extended to anything that is good. The mature Christian is one who loves good food, good music, good art, good literature. God is the creator of all good things and anything that is good, in some way, points to Him.

Sensible

This is a word that is also translated "sober." It combines the words for "wisdom" and "mindedness", so this is a "wise-minded" person. It has the sense of someone who is not flippant or silly. It does not mean that a mature Christian has no sense of humor. It simply means that the mature Christian is not silly or foolish. It also means someone who is not easily swayed by the pleasures or passions of the world.

Just

This could be interpreted two ways. It can mean someone who is just and fair in their own personal lives, and the way that they run their lives, or it can mean someone who can be trusted to judge fairly in all things. This would be someone who would not judge quickly based on prejudices or divisiveness. Both concepts certainly apply to the mature believer, and even more so to the qualified church leader. This person is just in their own personal lives but can also judge well in matters of the church.

Devout

This word means someone that is dedicated. This describes someone who is consciously trying to choose a path and a way that will please God. This person, in all areas of life, is acting in a way that is specifically to please God. This is one who is characterized by their resting in Christ and abiding in Him.

Self-Controlled

Self-control is one of the aspects of the fruit of the Spirit in Galatians 5:23. It does not mean Paul is asking us to be "self-helpers" or trying to do these things from our own power or might, but it is something that comes out of the work of the indwelling Holy Spirit. This is a result of the Spirit's work, not the result of our labor and efforts to control our actions. Just as a healthy vine does not have to "try" to make fruit, so a healthy believer will naturally exhibit these things as the Word is read and applied and as the believer is brought to maturity. However, the fruit of the spirit manifests itself as a person who is not out of control. We know when a person flies into a fit of rage, or under the control of a substance, that they are no longer exhibiting self-control, and this is **not** the character of the mature believer.

Verse 9

*...**holding fast the faithful word** which is in accordance with the teaching, so that he will be able both to **exhort in sound doctrine** and to **refute those who contradict**.*

The Shift

There is a shift in gears again between verses eight and nine. It moves from focusing on the characteristics of a godly leader to considering the abilities that are most central to the task of biblical eldership.

Holding Fast the Faithful Word

"Holding fast" could also be translated "clinging to." It pictures someone who is holding tight to doctrinal truth, not abandoning it for false doctrines. The ability of an elder is to be *very* concerned with good doctrine being at the center of the church and his life. The first purpose of the elder is to accurately teach biblical truth. This means that the elder is first a teacher. Not a counselor, nor a great public speaker, but a teacher. Someone who can teach from the Scriptures reliably without inserting private ideas but letting the Word of God speak for itself. Note the primacy of this function when discussing the actual "work" of the elder. The elder is not a designated hand-holder, visitor, cheerleader, or visionary. He clings to the word.

Exhort in Sound Doctrine

Empowered by "holding fast to the faithful word" the elder will have the ability to complete his other duties. Exhorting in sound doctrine means calling others to follow the Bible. This means *not* watering down the truth of the Word! *Not* avoiding things that conflict with the culture. It means taking a stand against everything that is not Biblical and boldly teaching the church to follow the Word of God and not the murmurings of popular science or psychology, or any other lies of the modern culture. Rather, the elder calls the believers to God's standard by the explanation and teaching of the Bible. This is not delivering shallow "Sunday pick-me-up" sermons, but by teaching the Word of God.

Refute Those Who Contradict

Only if the elder is steeped in this doctrinal soundness can he refute those who contradict. Immature Christians are easily swayed by any popular thing that is labeled as "Christian." It is the elder who should have his eyes on the horizon to protect to church from the lies of the world and the culture, and especially the lies of the false teachers who would claim to be Christians!

As Christians, we are to be concerned with attaining "the unity of the faith" (Eph 4:13). It is the job of the elder to identify divisive people and work towards correcting them, putting them out of the fellowship, if necessary (Tit 3:10).

TITUS 1:10–13

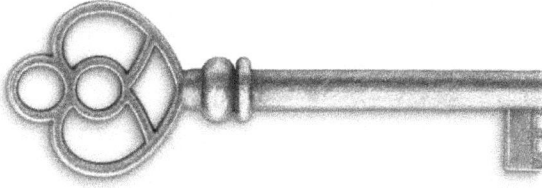

False Teachers

Paul has greeted Titus (Tit 1:1–4) and has given the requirements for elders (Tit 1:5–9) and now he is starting a new topic. This section tells, in great part, *why* the office of elder is so important, and *why* the Bible has standards for the character and equipment/gifting of the elders. This section is about false teachers. We must remember that in verse 9 Paul told us that elders need to be "holding fast the faithful word as he has been taught, that he may be able, by sound doctrine, both to exhort and convict those who contradict." This is to say that elders must be steeped in the Word, and well-trained in solid doctrine so that they can see the heresies of the world, of the culture, and of the multitude of false teachers that stream forth from so called "Christian media."

The elder needs to be in conflict with the cultural compromises made towards popular psychology (a man centered view of life, giving lies about "self-esteem" and "emotional conditions") , the church growth movements (popular movements that try to make it seem like the focus of churches should be to get more people in the door, rather than equip those who are already there), and the "prosperity gospel" (the belief that following God and being a Christian will result in material gain, or any sort of financial stability). The biblical elder must stand against the winds of all kinds of false teachers: both legalists and licentious abusers of grace, and those who teach false gospels like Lordship Salvation, or the prophecy fanatics and date-setters. The elder needs to have an eye out to dispel these lies, and fight for the truth of the Word of God. Boldly teaching, not afraid that some will leave, not afraid of losing his job because he didn't keep people happy, but boldly teaching the word of God—*especially* when it is uncomfortable! The sheep will always be drawn toward the diseased waters of popular false teachers in the form of books, radio, television, and internet broadcasts. The undiscerning will frequently find themselves trapped in false doctrines that pervert the clarity of the gospel, the truth of the blessed hope, and the healthy

27

doctrines that bring forth true spiritual growth. It is one of the more unpleasant, but important tasks of the elder today to make sure that people are warned against false teachers by name, movement, and false theology.

Verse 10

*For there are many **rebellious men, empty talkers** and **deceivers**, especially those of the **circumcision**...*

The Three Characteristics

Paul puts forth three common characteristics of false teachers:

1. **Rebellious**—This word can mean disobedient or unsubmitted. This word indicates that these teachers are of the kind of character that does not recognize authority. They are rebellious against the Word of God, as well as against the true spiritual authority of biblical eldership.

2. **Empty Talkers**—The Greek word here is *anupotaktos*. This word has the idea of empty, or fruitless and aimless chatter. Zodhaites writes: "It is building houses on sand, chasing the wind, shooting at stars, pursuing one's own shadow."[4] There is a self-centeredness implied in this. These are those who want to have endless empty discussion or air all their grievances. They are not doing anything edifying or constructive; they are only making a wasteful clamber.

3. **Deceivers**—This comes from the word *phrenapates*. It is made up of the two words: the word for "mind" and the word for "deceive." These are people who will try to pervert the minds of others with lies. In this context it can often mean people who have lied so much, or been lied to

---

[4] Spiros Zodhiates, ed. *The Complete Word Study Dictionary: New Testament*, Revised, Accordance electronic edition, version 1.3 (Chattanooga, TN: AMG Publishers, 1993).

so much, that they *believe* the lies that they are telling. It is possible for someone to be a deceiver who does not believe that they are lying. These people may be well intentioned, but they are still deceiving others and must be dealt with directly and decisively.

Circumcision

"Those of the circumcision" refers to those who followed Paul around trying to convince new believers that they had to be circumcised and obey Old Testament law to be saved. These were the people that Paul wrote against in Galatians and in Philippians 3:2: warning them to "beware of those dogs, those mutilators of the flesh." These wanted to make grace-saved Christians slaves to the principle of law. These people are still in our midst. These days they do always not demand circumcision, but they make new laws and legalisms for the Church to follow, claiming "you are not saved unless…" or "you aren't going to be sanctified until…" Legalism is still, as it was then, one of the most venomous and lethal influences that can destroy a church body.

Verse 11

*…who **must be silenced** because they **are upsetting** whole families, teaching things they should not teach for **the sake of sordid gain**.*

Must Be Silenced

In the original text this is a command – an imperative. This command is not a polite recommendation. It is something that absolutely must be done for the local church to magnify Christ on this earth. This is like a teacher in a classroom, or a judge in a court of law, commanding someone to be silent at once! The word in Greek here is *epistomizo*. It is another compound word combining the words for "over" or "cover" and the word for "mouth." So literally it would read "cover their mouths." Or "shove something in their mouths." The picture of shoving a piece of cloth in a person's mouth, and then putting duct-tape over the cloth is not too extreme a picture of this concept. Paul is not using childish language, nor polite language. This is his charge to elders: not to baby these types of people but to silence them.

Here we see again that the elder is not to be just a "nice guy." The biblical leader is supposed to be tough, and tell things like they are, according to the Word of God, regardless of the consequences. This is also further evidence that our vision of "tolerance" is not to be accepted in the realm of different doctrines. Here again it is clear that the church is not to be a hodgepodge of "some say this, and some say that" but rather to be clinging to God's truth in a clear and uniform way.

Upsetting

This word in the Greek means literally "to overturn, or to turn upside-down." These teachers aren't just causing minor problems. These false teachers are destroying groups of people. Many so-called pastors today will take a liberal view of doctrine, downplaying its importance. Paul is very clear: Bad teaching turns whole households upside-down. They are confusing people. This is something that we take for granted in our culture. Bad information destroys people. Legalistic teaching, if tolerated, will destroy believers, and keep them from "growing in the grace and knowledge of the Lord Jesus Christ." Legalistic or licentious believers will not glorify God and make Jesus Christ known according to God's design. Paul is serious about this because it is the difference between the church fulfilling the purpose of bringing glory to God in the world through bringing believers to maturity, and believers who fall from grace and become useless to the Lord. The elders need to be against this!

Families

The word translated "family" here is literally "houses." It could very well mean that families were being thrown into confusion by these false teachers and idle talkers. However, at this time church meetings were also held in homes. This could also take on the meaning that entire churches were being thrown into confusion as well, because of the elders' lack of scriptural training and understanding. Notice also how high the stakes are: these houses are being destroyed, people are being denied the opportunity to behold the Lord Jesus Christ and be transformed from glory to glory. If someone misunderstands their toaster instructions and thinks that the pictures mean that it was meant to be used in the bathtub there is going to be a serious problem. The spiritual problems are even more pressing, and broken fellowship (not relationship) with the Lord can be the result.

The Sake of Sordid Gain

They are teaching things that they should not be teaching. Bad things, wrong things, or things that are not consistent with Scripture, things that are not found in Scripture. They are teaching these things to get money. "Sordid" here means "shameful and repulsive." It is dirty gain; it is disgusting profit. There are countless popular speakers getting paid a fortune to go from church to church with their popular lies. Finding out the net-worth of a so called "minister" or popular Christian personality can be an excellent way to find their true motivation. Their money, their gain, is forever stained.

The pastor who is preaching to make his congregation happy should beware of this message. If he is not boldly proclaiming the Word of God regardless of what the people want, regardless of what gets more people in the door, then he is merely trying to keep his job. The Bible is clear that elders are not accountable to men alone, but to God. By subjecting himself to the authority of his congregation he is disobeying the word of God and doing that congregation an immeasurable disservice. Any pastor or elder "preaching" happy, non-threatening little "sermonettes" on Sundays is watering down God's Word, for the sake of his own filthy gain.

Additionally, the pastor using legalism to pressure people into giving more money or participate in the church is repulsive. This is a great temptation to church leaders as guilt gets things done, and by way of guilt and coercion the earthly goals of a pastor may be fulfilled. However, the church should be concerned with God's goals, not human goals. Relying on Him, not guilt or shame, to make things happen.

Verse 12

*One of themselves, a **prophet** of their own, said, "Cretans are always **liars, evil beasts, lazy gluttons**."*

The Cretan Condition

The introduction section discussed the character of Crete and Cretans. They were pirates and thieves. Their entire culture was built upon deception, admiring the traitor and the cheater. They would pray to their gods to help them to cheat, lie and deceive more effectively. Paul is telling us that the culture of Crete is already predisposed for making these kinds of people (false teachers, idle talkers, deceivers). And that the people would be desensitized to it and may not easily recognize these people for who they were.

Prophet

By "prophet" Paul does not mean a Biblical prophet. He is not comparing this poet to Isaiah or Jeremiah, but in this generic sense it means "wise man" or "philosopher." Many have identified this poet as Epimenides, a Cretan poet before the New Testament era.

Liars

The Greek word here is *pseustes* meaning "liar." It is where we get the English word "pseudo." We use this as a prefix to mean that something is false. So, a "pseudo-intellectual" only pretending to be intellectually equipped. This is another similarity between Cretan culture and modern western culture. An hour of modern advertising is an hour of lies, misdirection, and deception. All entertainment is exclusively lies and deceptions, and modern politicians lie so readily they no longer have any sense of truth at all. This culture of lies is often justified by the fact that everyone knows that we are surrounded by lies of every kind. Even if everyone knows, lies are still in conflict with the character of God.

Evil Beasts

Evil beasts here means that they are uncontrollable. The Cretans cannot be tamed, or controlled, they are unpredictable. They are like wild animals. This does not necessarily mean they are uncivilized by a worldly perspective. They undoubtedly found as many ways as modern culture to justify their wicked tendencies. In the modern world we see the uncontrolled proliferation of sexual immorality, pornography, and human trafficking as only a few examples of the enslavement of the modern world to the most base and ungodly passions and desires.

Lazy Gluttons

This means that they are also the type to try to get out of work. That is the purpose of their cheating and lying. They can take it easy and not have to work anymore. They are freeloaders. What hope does the church have with these types of people around? The hope, as we will see, is in the continual steadfast teaching of the word. This, again, is found in the in modern culture as well. Use of technology to escape any kind of labor, or productivity of any kind has made a culture of grown adults who would rather watch a movie or play a video game than truly produce anything. The cultural tendency towards obesity also seems to offer evidence that this Cretan attitude has become the attitude of the modern west as well. This kind of sloth is not only unwise, but ungodly.

Verse 13

This testimony is true. For this reason reprove them severely so that they may be sound in the faith…

This Testimony is True

Wow! This is shocking! Paul doesn't water it down; Paul doesn't suggest that Titus and the elders he appoints should be "sensitive to their culture." It simply says that it's the truth! The word for testimony here focuses on verifiable, visible evidence. Saying, "you can go check it for yourself." And for this reason, Titus and the elders are told to…

Reprove Them Severely

Reprove means "to rebuke or to censure." Titus was to confront them and tell them that they are off the mark. He is not simply to hope it goes away in time or hope that they improve, but to rebuke them. Severely here is a compound word using the words for "from" and "cut sharply." This is a decisive, harsh, and serious action. He is to act harshly in response to the culture. Titus is commanded to tell them to leave their culture for it is not of God! Culture is not a sacred thing! Human culture is the destroyer of local churches and theology throughout the generations. Culture does not need to be considered but disregarded in favor of our new heavenly citizenship.

Sound in the Faith

Why should they do this? Why do we need to fight the culture? Why do elders need to be constantly on the lookout? Because the lies of the culture are in opposition to soundness of faith. They make an unsound faith. They prevent the people in the church from reaching spiritual maturity. They are not to be rebuked sharply to make Titus feel better, nor are they to be rebuked because elders should like to fight. They need to be rebuked for their own good. For their own soundness of faith. This term has also been translated "healthiness of faith."

This is a beautiful image of the church functioning well. A healthy church has individual believers who have healthy beliefs. Think of the metaphor comparing physical health and spiritual health. As a physically healthy person can move, work, play, rest and live; so, a healthy faith is one that provides the believer with the ability to live a free and healthy life, eat, work, serve, know, and love the Lord in everything.

TITUS 1:14–16

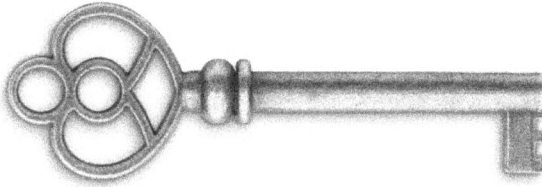

Verse 14

...not paying attention to Jewish myths and commandments of men who turn away from the truth.

Not Paying Attention

Here is another apparent command: "Don't pay attention to…" In the Greek grammar we find that this is a participle, which is well translated here. The present participle gives the idea of continuing present action. We could view it as a weak imperative. Not weak in the sense that we may disregard it if we want, but weak in the sense that it lacks the force of the imperative mood. It is a command that communicates that Paul assumes that Titus is already doing this.

Notice that the exhortation here is to "not pay attention" or stated more positively, "ignore." Notice that there is a distinction from our culture here. Modern thinking would recommend that everyone should get a say, that every viewpoint should be considered. The point here is that believers in Crete were *not* to give these false teachers an audience, and that the Jewish myths should be simply ignored, not searched through for some "hidden value" as we see many doing today.

Jewish Myths

The Jewish myths that Paul was talking about are well known to us these days. The books of the Apocrypha (that are still found in the Catholic Bible) are not to be regarded as Scripture at all. The books involved in that body of literature are mostly fictional accounts written long after the facts. They are not regarded by Jews as sacred but only the Catholic and Eastern Orthodox Churches. The Catholic Church seems to cleave to them because they support the idea of being able to give money to forgive sin (a practice of the Catholic Church, historically). However, they are fictional accounts posing as Biblical history. They include various spells and superstitions that, while part of cultural Judaism of the time, was not reflected in Scripture.

There is also a great deal of "apocalyptic" Jewish literature around this time. These were long drawn-out Jewish accounts of what Hell would be like and what would happen to people in Hell. Other books had a morbid level of interest in the unseen world and encouraged readers to be overly concerned with the movements and actions of angels and demons. They were made to scare people, and they were not inspired literature. They were the Jewish myths that are very attractive to people because they are *mystical* and *secret,* and people love feeling like they have a bit of "secret" knowledge that no one else has. These documents have ebbed and flowed in public interest over time, and they are often the source of information for false teachers even to this day. Such myths do not edify the believer. They have value as ancient historical documents that reveal much about the ancient Jewish world, but they do not provide trustworthy spiritual information.

It should be noted that this heresy is in current circulation today. Many are working to try to include the Apocrypha in protestant Bibles and Study Bibles. One example of this is "The Spiritual Formation Study Bible." While there are several cautions and reasons not to even consider this work, one is that they place these "Jewish myths" on par with Scripture by placing them directly in the middle of the text.

Commandments of Men

These are extra laws or legalism as given by men. These kinds of commandments were probably dietary commandments. Like the Judaizers (those of the circumcision party) who would tell the Gentile Christians that they should not eat the foods that are forbidden by the Old Testament Law or that they should observe the Sabbath. It would also be people who went around claiming that they should not eat meat, or drink wine. This legalism has been plaguing the church since her birth in Acts 2. It manifests itself in petty abstinence from dancing, popular music, bowling, or the cinema and make such judgments about any other non-moral issue. Getting caught up in the commandments of men takes our eyes off our Savior and inevitably brings only destruction and the urging of Scripture is to ignore these extra, unbiblical, man-made standards.

Turn Away from the Truth

These men (or people) who give these types of commandments have turned away from the truth. Turning from the truth is part of their character. They are not seeking after the truth or clinging to it, but they have turned away from it, making a legalism of their own for their own self-righteousness and self-approval.

Verse 15

*To **the pure, all things are pure**; but to those who are **defiled and unbelieving, nothing is pure**, but both their **mind and their conscience** are defiled.*

The Pure

This declaration of the believer as "pure" comes from the position that Christ has put the believer. When someone believes in Jesus Christ, trusting Him alone for salvation, that person is put "in Christ." Romans 6:3–11 describes this process clearly. God positions the believer in Christ, it is God's will, not man's will that puts him there. In this position of union with Jesus Christ, the believer is equipped with every spiritual blessing (Eph 1:3–14). That is the Christian's position. That is how the Christian is regarded. The believer is not pure because of what he or she has done, the believer is pure because of what Christ did.

All Things are Pure

This verse is *not* telling us that anything a Christian does is pure. This verse makes perfect sense in relation to the last phrase. There are going to be those saying, "don't do this, don't eat that, don't drink this, don't use that." There were even some early Gnostic cults that claimed that the physical universe was completely unclean and evil, that matter itself was evil, which is not the teaching of Scripture. To the person whom God has declared physically clean, the material world contains nothing that is impure. Not food, nor drink, nor any other legalism that someone may want to add to Scripture. This is giving the theological basis as to why legalism is silly: it is inconsistent with the truth that God has revealed in relation to our identity and position in Christ.

Defiled and Unbelieving

Defile means to be stained with color, like glass, or fabric. This means those who are stained, morally polluted, and corrupted. The verb tense here suggests that they have been polluted in the past and they are continuing to be more polluted to this day. This is a picture of the unsaved person. The sin nature can do nothing pure. The unsaved person can provide no good work. Even with the best tools and most righteous starting place they are stained and defiled.

Nothing is Pure

So, to these people nothing is pure at all. Nothing good is going to come out of them. They are too defiled; they should not be listened to. We might say "Garbage in, garbage out!" We could imagine a very dirty baking dish which is caked with motor oil, filth, and mud. Anything prepared in that dish will wind up being nothing but dirty! Sure, the chicken, potatoes and cheese were clean going in, but only disgustingly filthy food came out. To the defiled and unbelieving nothing is pure.

Mind and Conscience

Paul is clear that even their minds and their consciences are seared. Their consciences still bear witness that they are not in the right, but they have been ruined and beaten into submission by their defiled and unbelieving actions. The mind is, of course, the seat of intellect where judgments are made based on incoming facts. The conscience is the internal judge of right and wrong. In the unbeliever neither faculty is functioning according to their design. They are stained, ruined, no longer useful.

Verse 16

*They **profess** to **know** God, but by their **deeds they deny** Him, being **detestable and disobedient and worthless for any good deed**.*

Profess

This word for "profess" is a compound word. It combines the words "same" and "word." So, these people are "same-wording" that they know

God. They are claiming to know God. Here is the great irony in the life of the legalist: he *thinks* he knows God better because of his good works and his abstinence from this or that non-moral issue. The sad irony continues in that the world and most of "Christendom" has decided that this is correct. Manmade Christianity looks at the legalist and says, "My! Isn't he holy?" When the reality is that none could be further from the heart of God!

Know

This word for "know" focuses on a kind of knowing that is personal, intuitive knowledge that has come by perception. These people are claiming to know God in a very intuitive way, a very personal way, they are not just claiming to know about God.

Deeds They Deny

By their works and their actions, they are denying God. They say one thing about who God is and what He demands of us, but then they deny Him by their actions. It is important to realize that there should be a deep connection in the life of any elder between what he teaches and how he lives his life. Keep in mind the legalist is trying to save or sanctify himself by good works. Paul is saying that these very good works deny Christ. By their attempts to earn or preserve their salvation they deny that He needed to go to the cross: "I do not set aside the grace of God; for if righteousness comes through the law, then Christ died in vain" (Gal 2:10).

Detestable, Disobedient and Worthless

Paul is filled with disgust for these who were ruining the churches all over Crete. Disgusted with their lies and hypocrisy, he declares them positively horrid; saying that they are detestable (which could also be translated "sickening"), disobedient, and *worthless* for good work. This means that they are incapable of doing any truly good deed. It does not mean that they can't do kind things, or right things like giving to the poor, or helping the sick, but it means that everything that comes out of them is defiled and cannot be called "good" because it is not from God. Their works are *not* those of Ephesians 2:10.

TITUS 2:1–2

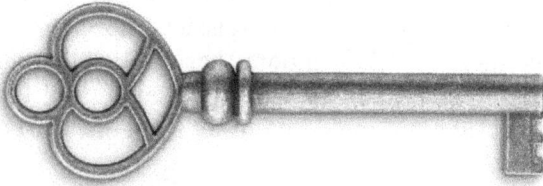

Instructions for Godly Living

Paul is changing directions again here. Paul first greeted Titus and told him a bit about his mission. Next, he explained the qualifications for the office of eldership. This revealed what character traits should be present in a believer who is mature. Then Paul warned Titus against false teachers that would plague the Church by trying to put them under law or deceive them into following another way.

Now Paul is back onto the positive. He has accurately described the character of the people of Crete, but he doesn't dwell on it. He recognizes it, but then moves forward with the way they should act due to the Holy Spirit's great work within them. He now starts by talking about each demographic. He follows the basic order of:

1. Older Men (2:2)

2. Older Women (2:3)

3. Younger Women (2:4–5)

4. Younger Men (2:6–8)

5. Slaves (2:9–10)

Verse 1

But as for you, speak *the things which are fitting for* ***sound doctrine.***

But as for You

Paul is drawing a strong contrast. He just talked about the horrible works of the false teachers and has denounced them completely in saying that they are completely unfit to do *any* good work. Everything these false teachers touch is horribly corrupted by bad motive and bad doctrine. The Holy Spirit is quite clear that there is to be a stark distinction between the lives of the false teachers and the lives of the Church.

Speak

This is in the present tense meaning that is something that is meant to happen in the current time. We know imperatives quite well. We hear them every day. "Take out the trash." "Make sure you get this task done before you clock out today." "Do this before lunch!" It is not a question, nor is it a suggestion. It is a command. It is important to understand commands in the Pauline sense. Paul these imperatives are not motivated by threats of any kind. Paul is rather saying, "Jesus has done a good work in you and as He lives His life out in you, and expresses Himself through you, it is imperative that you realize that speaking bad doctrine is inconsistent with who you are in Christ." Paul is showing these people who have been lied to by their cultures what is and isn't consistent with who they are in Christ.

Sound

This word translated "sound" can mean "sound, whole, to be whole, wholesome, and healthy." Believers' communication is to be whole and healthy. This obviously includes things that are good doctrine. "Doctrine" is a word that has received a great deal of misunderstanding, and many mainline churches today are trying to stay away from the concept of doctrine for fear of offending someone or putting people off. The reality is that the Bible is not impossibly difficult to understand. If believers choose to take Scripture at face value, then resultant living will abound with good doctrine. This means that Christians must be careful and observant readers of Scripture because they don't want to do or believe anything that opposes the Bible.

This excludes at least two types of communication: 1—unsound, or unhealthy teaching which contradicts the Bible. And 2—(indirectly) the kind of talk that is degrading. This includes filthy language, cursing, and abusive language; and certainly, excludes all manner of gossip.

Doctrine

The word "doctrine" simply means teaching. When we talk about doctrine, we are talking about the things we believe based on the Bible. It is common to hear people say that they don't wish to talk about doctrine, because doctrine divides. However, these have already established that their doctrine (the teaching that they follow) is not to look, learn, or observe the teaching (doctrine) of the Bible. This word has turned into something of a straw man for divisive and hurtful words and behavior in the church…which is the result of bad doctrine! Understand, this is not to say it is all the fault of those people who don't see things a certain way. Good and bad doctrine has been communicated in ways that are divisive and uncharitable. Splits are tragically made over non-essential issues which are vague or unclear in Scripture. It is bad doctrine not "to speak the truth in love" as Ephesians commands. Believers are to speak the truth and to do so in love. There is not a tension between truth and love. Speaking the truth is a loving act; if done without love it is wrong, even if the point being made is correct. Hiding from doctrine is not a solution, it just causes greater problems. Bad doctrine is the problem and healthy doctrine is the answer.

On the divisive nature of doctrine, an important point must be made: a good doctrinal statement should cause divisions! Good doctrine is what separates orthodox Christianity from the cults such as the Mormons and Jehovah's Witnesses. Good doctrine separates true believers from those who hold to anti-trinitarian heresies and the delusion that they are receiving revelation directly from God. A good doctrinal statement weeds out who does and doesn't really believe what the Bible says.

A good example is the issue of baptism, which is often controversial. The controversy is over a very important issue. If someone believes that they are somehow saved by baptism, then they obviously don't believe that they are saved by grace through faith in Christ. That person believes that the act, or work, of baptism is what saved them. There is a strong implication in Scripture (specifically in the Epistle to the Galatians) that if you believe that you will be saved by any works (whether baptism, circumcision, communion, or good deeds) then you haven't trusted fully in Christ and may never have been saved. Do people with bad doctrinal beliefs need to be catered to or corrected? What is the most loving course of action? Clearly, speaking the truth is the only loving response.

Verse 2

Older men are to be temperate, dignified, sensible, sound in faith, in love, in perseverance.

Older men

The word for "older men" here is *presbutes* it is the same root word that is translated "elder" in other contexts. The fact that the passage is talking about the whole Church in general here leads us to believe that this is referring not exclusively to those who hold the office of elder, but to all the older Christian men here.

It shows us another snapshot of Christian maturity. It shows us what it looks like when Christ is at work in the life of an older believer. We need to study this because it is God's plan that we are moving closer to this model every day!

To Be

We see the word "to be" here in the present tense. These character qualities have their place in the present. We must assume that if the Lord makes a command for these things in the present tense that they must be possible in the present tense as we rest in Jesus Christ and His word. We need not view these things as the impossible standard that none will attain, but as the things we can naturally expect to flow out of our lives as we live in union with Christ Jesus.

Temperate

This word can mean "temperate", "well-balanced" or it could also be translated as "sober." It has both the meaning of someone who is not drunken, and of someone who has a good perspective on things.

Dignified

This is how the older men are to be carrying themselves. It has also been translated "grave" "honorably" and "seriously." This is not to say that Christian maturity is to have no sense of humor. But it is about being honorable and showing integrity in even the smallest areas of life. The Christian must remember the dignity of his or her position in Christ. It is easy to be motivated by the desire for approval or admiration of others, and this can bring about all kinds of ungodly actions and attitudes. We do well to remember this as we walk through our daily lives.

Sensible

This is a compound word built out of the word *sophos*, meaning wisdom, from which we get the word "philosophy" (i.e., the love of wisdom) and the word *freneo* meaning mind. This is a wise minded person. It also carries with it the sense of one who has denounced the pleasures of this world as the source of their joy and life. It is not to be understood as demanding aestheticism—not eating any good food or enjoying any good entertainment—it is a wise, moderated use of those things which does not approach idolatry. This is the part of maturity that does not seek comfort or distraction in the pleasures of this world but seeks comfort in our relationship with Jesus Christ.

Sound

"Sound" is the verb for the last three elements of the spiritually mature, physically older man's character. Just as in the previous verse it means whole and healthy. It means that the believer is to be whole and complete in faith, whole and complete in love, and whole and complete in perseverance. Notice that the constant focus of Paul here is the concept of health. The goal of good doctrine is spiritual health. If a believer is spiritually, or emotionally unhealthy then it is the beliefs of that person which must be first examined.

Faith

In the Greek we find that the definite article (the word "the") is present in this phrase. This is not just "sound in faith" but rather "sound in *the* Faith." When the definite article is used in the Greek it means the specific thing that is being talked about. This is not faith generally, not any faith, or faith in anything, but the specific faith that was taught by the Apostles and Prophets in the Bible. The specific teachings. This is another reference to the importance of knowing what the Bible teaches.

44

Christianity is not meant to be a life of constant shoulder shrugging and uncertainty but the security that results from understanding of the Bible. Every believer is to be mature in the faith and the knowledge of the Word. This is not to be limited to pastors, teachers, and elders. It is every single believer that needs to know what the bible teaches!

Love

Here the Apostle uses the Greek word *agape*. God's love. This love is unconditional and sourced in the Lord alone. This is not something that humans can contrive or make up or try to generate within the emotional capacity. Rather, believers must be healthy in God's unconditional, saving, perfect *agape* love. This love that constantly looks to the best interests of the one who is loved, regardless of the cost to the lover. It is a love that surpasses what this world knows of love or believes about love. It is something that can only be found in the God of the Bible.

Perseverance

This word literally means "to remain under." It could also be translated "be patient." It has to do with dealing with every ordeal and situation with a courageous and abiding staying power that is not easily torn away, or not abandoning a difficult situation. It is a trait that is needed in a life that will face longstanding trials with courage, knowing that God's glory is the very reason for each passing day.

TITUS 2:3–5

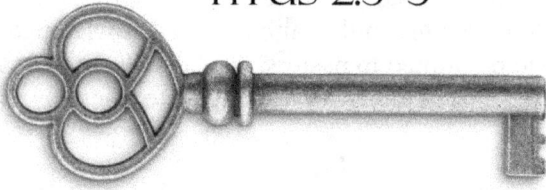

Verse 3

Older women likewise are to be reverent in their behavior, not malicious gossips nor enslaved to much wine, teaching what is good…

Older Women

This word, in Greek, is *presbutidas*. It comes from the same word as *older men* in the last verse we looked at, only this is in the feminine meaning "older women." This is a sect of society that often feels neglected and mistreated. Many older women today, as in Paul's day, feel worthless or useless. Society views the elderly, particularly the elderly women as an inconvenience. This is not God's design for the Church. The Lord recognizes the immeasurable value of the elderly, particularly elderly women. These verses explore vital importance of older women in the mission of the local church.

Likewise

This word is *hosautos*. It means "in like manner, or in the same way." So here we see older women being held to the same character traits as the older men. The standards for women are not less than those for men. There are no value statements in the Bible that say women are of less value or held to a lesser spiritual standard. The modern accusation that the Bible, by differentiating between the sexes, is putting value statements on them is a slanderous falsehood. Nothing could be further from the truth.

Reverent

This is a very interesting word in Greek. It is a compound word, combining the words for "to be holy" and the word for "to be conspicuous, fit." The women are to be conspicuous in their holiness. Just like all Christians, they are not to conform to the culture around them, nor are they to behave in the manner of the examples that are set before them in the media or in history. They are to be marked by a holiness that sets them apart and makes them visibly and noticeably different from the culture.

Malicious Gossips

This Greek word here is *diabolos*. It is the origin of the English word "Devil," and it is used to describe Satan in Scripture. The KJV translates this "false accusers," this is the trait of a person that heeds rumors as well as passes them on, even making them up! This is rightly compared to an evil or fiendish behavior as it destroys the credibility, reputation, and image of others without any due cause. This is a special trap that woman often struggle with more than men; however, that is not to say at all that men cannot be involved in this sort of behavior. It is expressly forbidden by Scripture.

Enslaved to Much Wine

In dealing with both the idea of malicious gossips and drunkenness, the Apostle Paul approaches two very common pitfalls for elderly women. It was very common in Paul's day that older women who were culturally stripped of their value and purpose in society would turn to drink or become busybodies. This is something that is still true today. Tragically, the trend of glorifying excessive wine consumption in older women has become a tragic cultural phenomenon. In pointing these out Paul is discouraging the women from making poor lifestyle choices because the Lord esteems them so highly. God's word instills them with such an important mission in the functioning of the Church. He rests a huge and most valuable portion of the Church on their shoulders.

Teaching What is Good

This phrase translates one big compound word that is a noun rather than a verb. It would be better rendered "teachers of good." For they are to be teachers of good things. This is critical because it means that women are to have good doctrine too. So often doctrine gets categorized as a "guy thing." This isn't to say that everyone who is not able or interested in learning Greek or systematic theology is not a true believer, but it is to say that what the women teach is important and should be in keeping with good doctrine, which means that the women must strive to know that their doctrine is from Scripture and not from any other source.

Verse 4

*...so **that they may encourage** the young women to **love their husbands**, to **love their children**,*

That They May

The translation seems to imply that they might, or they might not. Usually when the translation reads "that they may" or "that you might" it does not imply that it may not happen, but rather that it is meant to happen. This is not saying that the elderly women may encourage the younger women if they want, but rather that they should be about the business of building up the younger women.

Encourage

In Greek, this word has the idea of encouraging someone to their personal duty. The older women are to teach the young women. It is very interesting the older women are given the responsibility to teach, care for, and discipline the younger women. This is very important, especially today. It is not usually appropriate for a male elder to council a young woman, especially in a one-on-one setting. This is something that Paul gives to the older women to oversee. This implies appropriate relationships between men and women who are not married to one another. Even if nothing inappropriate happens it can raise questions in the minds of onlookers and mar the credibility of the church. This is a massively important task that can only be correctly managed by the older women.

Love Their Husbands

The young women are to be taught and encouraged to be "lovers of their husbands." There is an interesting point here in the Greek. The word for love here in the Greek is *phileo* which can denote a brotherly love, or (in this case) a responsive love. In both Ephesians and Colossians, husbands are called to love their wives with *agape* love. This is the love that comes with God as its source. It is the husband's responsibility, in a Christian household, to be pouring that love into the home. The woman's love for her husband is reciprocal based on that love that the Christian husband bestows. This does not, however, mean that women whose husbands are not living up to their potential are off the hook. That is why the older women are so important in their encouragement of the younger women to love their families.

This choice of words is remarkable because it is not the erotic love that would be expressed by *eros*. It is a caring and compassionate love. Paul minces no words that marriage is not just butterflies in the stomach, blushing, and physical attraction. But is a lifelong dedication and caring love that goes far beyond that portrayed by any romance movie.

Love Their Children

This word is like the word before it. However, this combines the words *phileo* (love) and *teknon* (Children), so the older women are to encourage the younger women to be lovers of their children. This insinuates a love that cares for the children and puts the children before herself. This takes encouragement. This is a love that endures faithfully and cares for the needs of her children, and it relies upon the instruction and encouragement from the older women.

Verse 5

...to be **sensible, pure, workers at home**, *kind, being* **subject to** *their own husbands, so that the* **word of God will not be dishonored**.

Sensible

This word means "wise-minded." It also implies chastity and modesty. It describes a person who is self-controlled and has an eternal perspective over what is good for the children and good for her family, including what is constructive and what is destructive. This is a wisdom that rejects foolishness and quietly builds up the family.

Pure

This word can mean purity from specifically carnal sins, as well as a general righteousness. This is, of course, not some pie in the sky demand to be made of wives, but a general area in which they are growing in character. This is not to say that they never sinned before, or never make mistakes, but rather that they are right now growing in this purity that is the natural outflow of their position in Christ.

Workers at Home

It is one of the great tragedies of the modern worldview which places a low value on keeping the home. Often women who are wives and mothers are viewed as not having as much drive or not having goals. This is a gross lie. The family is the first human institution that God instated. The keeping and caring for that union is one of the highest callings in all of humanity. Satan has used every tool available to debase this role and tear the family apart by belittling its chief cornerstone: the wife.

Subject to

This is another word that has a horrible connotation in modern times. The Greek word is *hupotasso* combining the word for "under" with the word for "attach." It is also in the passive voice. The wife is to be supportively attached to her husband. Holding him up and supporting him as the spiritual leader of the family. This does not mean that the wife is a doormat. It is important to observe that in this passage, Ephesians 5:22–33 and Colossians 3:18–19, the wives are told to submit (this word "under-attach") to their husbands, and the word for obedience is never used. In addition to this, husbands are not told to force her to submit. This submission does not mean blindly following, God's plan for the family is that the wife has her say as well, but the final decision rests on the husband's shoulders.

Word of God Will Not Be Dishonored

Is it really all that important? Yes! If this command is ignored, then the Church dishonors (KJV "blasphemes") the word of God. It is dishonored amongst the family, among the Church, and before the unbelieving world. This should be the foremost consideration in family life, choice of spouse, and making decisions about conduct and expectations within the home.

TITUS 2:6–8

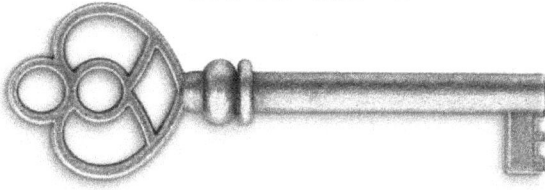

For the Young Men

Here Paul turns to the young men. This is another major group in society with a unique place in the local church. Some have thought that it was a bit strange that Paul didn't dedicate more instruction to the young men. Mal Couch, in his commentary,[5] suggests that this is perhaps because the culture of the time would already have put men in a place where they should be listening to their elders and acting obediently. However, we find that Paul gives precious pearls of wisdom to the young men here, which very likely also hit home with Titus as he was a young man himself.

Verse 6

Likewise urge the young men to be sensible.

Likewise

While gender and age do affect what is expected of us on a Biblical level, there is a very strong thread of consistency. The character requirements of Christian maturity are common to all the groups. Christ's life lived out in the lives of all believers has a similarity that cannot be denied.

Urge

This word, in the Greek, is another compound word: *parakaleo*. It combines the words *para* meaning "alongside" or "with", and *kaleo* meaning "to call." This is not a futile urging, nor a distant commanding, but rather one that says, "Walk alongside me." It is a personal and

---

[5] Mal Couch, *A Pastor's Manual on Doing Church: Pastor's Resource Commentary on Titus* (Buffalo, NY: Twenty-First Century Press, 2002).

demonstrated lifestyle. It says that the younger men need to be "called alongside" towards living out their position in Christ in a very practical way. This is the language of discipleship which should be the norm of the church body life.

Young Men

Different commentators have different opinions about the exact range of this word. Some have suggested that it only means those who are teenagers or late teenagers. There are other commentators who go to the complete opposite end and suggest that "young man" can refer to anyone under the age of 50 or 60. The definition that seems most appropriate, however, is that the young men are those who are still learning and growing, still pliable, and not yet hardened in their morality and their Christlikeness. This would suggest those who had not yet reached a maturity in Christ.

Sensible

Here again we see the word sensible. This word *sophroneo* has been applied to each of the groups thus far. It is obviously an important quality for exhibiting the life of Christ in the life of the believer. Once again, it combines the words for "wisdom" and "mindedness, or mindset." The very nature of the mindset should be one that is wise and balanced. This comes from having a solid biblical knowledge, applied in every situation. It has a circumspect view that sees what is going on and makes wise choices based on godly wisdom and submission to the Word and the Holy Spirit.

Verse 7

> ...*in all things show yourself* to be an *example* of *good deeds*, with *purity in doctrine, dignified*...

In All Things

The word for "all" in Greek is *panta* and it literally means *all* or *everything*. This is also where we get our English prefix "pan" as found in the word "pandemic." In this case it is preceded by the word *peri* meaning "around, about or concerning" and could be translated "in respect to all things." But the reality is that it is all inclusive. The special temptation of young men is to make exceptions based on circumstances. Perhaps one may think that excessive drinking is appropriate if the person is going through a difficult situation. Or another may believe his anger is justified because of circumstances and it is then acceptable to take it out on the object of that anger. However, Paul is putting forth a "no exceptions" lifestyle. This is in all things and in all ways that we are to be living in this manner.

Show Yourself

This verb "to show" is in the middle voice. That should be interpreted so that the subject (the young men) is very involved in the reflexive action. The young man is to be showing to the world what character the Lord is building into him. This is a display and a witness for everyone in the young man's life that people will notice. Not only so they can see and believe, but also so that non-believers won't have anything bad to say about Christianity as a whole. The Christian is, in a sense, always on display. The world knows who belongs to the Lord and they are looking for the evidence of His character in each of us.

Example

The Greek word translated "example" is *tupos* and is translated in the King James Version as "pattern." It is where we get our English word "type." There were no typewriters in Paul's time, however this was the word used of the impressions made by large stamps on metal and wood. A large stamp would be put on the thing to be embossed and hit with a large hammer to make a deep impression. The same picture (or type) would be made every single time, and every single stamp would be fully identical. This is what Christ wants for each believer, like a stamp of Him in each believer's day to day life.

Good Deeds

This is a good literal translation. It is important to note that the young men are to be examples of good works, not in order that salvation may be achieved, but as an outward testimony. There is no place in Scripture where works provide eternal salvation, or even add to salvation! The reality is that good works are to flow from a believer's inward relationship with Christ and will flow out of the Christian's life as a natural consequence of eternal union with Him. That said, it does not mean that we are off the hook in some way, we cannot sit around and wait for the good works to come. If they are not present in our lives we need to go to Christ and evaluate our relationship with Him, surrendering to Him anew and asking Him to produce fruit in our lives. Notice that Paul gives this message instructing young men to abound in good works to Titus, who was mature and knew the gospel, knowing that works would never save, or sanctify. He gave Titus this command with the knowledge that he would be able to convey the need clearly to the young men, that they would know the spiritual reality.

Purity in Doctrine

One common idea about purity is something that is dainty, or fragile. The pure cloth is so easily made impure. The concept in Greek is not just purity in doctrine, but rather a doctrinal incorruptibility. This is the man of God who knows what the Bible says, believes it, and will not be swayed by the winds of bad teaching or the world. Many believers are undiscriminating about their spiritual diet and are vulnerable to all manner of false beliefs. The goal is to grow to become someone who doesn't succumb to a bunch of rubbish and spiritual junk food. This is the man who is firm in his faith and is not easily swayed by the popular worldly influences that claim to be Christian. This person is not easily pulled away from the truth but seeks after a better understanding of what the Bible is saying. Again, it is made clear that doctrine is very important.

Dignified

Thayer's Lexicon[6] defines this Greek word as "the characteristic of a thing or person which entitles to reverence and respect, dignity, majesty, sanctity." There is a manner of *gravitas* that is being talked about here. This is a person who is not merely a goofball. It does not forbid a sense of humor; it merely means that the young men should conduct themselves with a gravity that can be taken seriously and does not make

---

[6] Joseph H. Thayer, *Thayer's Greek-English Lexicon of the New Testament* (Peabody, MA: Hendrickson Publishers Marketing, LLC, 2019), 573, n. 4587.

light of serious matters. Much as Christ's presence brought joy and wonder, but He was also not one that would be taken lightly.

Verse 8

*...**sound in speech** which is **beyond reproach**, so that the opponent will be **put to shame**, having **nothing bad to say about us**.*

Sound in Speech

The word "sound" appears yet again. Here, as before, it is defined as "healthy, whole, and sound." Furthermore, the word here translated as "speech" is a word that denotes the message, not simply the act of speaking, or the individual words spoken. This is to say that Christian speech needs to build others up and not tear down. The message of the believer's speech needs to be in keeping with sound doctrine and good words.

Beyond Reproach

This is one big word in Greek. The word is *akatagnostos* (try to say that three times fast). It is a compound word of three words: "*a*" which is a negative particle, *kata* which meant down on or against, and *gnosko* meaning knowledge or information. All together they mean "no-against-knowledge." That no one would have any knowledge or reasoning against a Christian.

Put to Shame

By good actions and good words, the enemies of the faith will be put to shame. By sound teaching and constant application of that doctrine, the people who write books and make their living opposing the Christian faith will be ashamed by the lives of believers. The witness of love is a powerful testimony in the sight of even the most gross and disgusting false accusation. This is the power of every believer who rests in Christ. As we walk in the Spirit the fruit of the Spirit will grow and will be recognized by unbelievers as a thing not of this world.

Nothing Bad to Say About Us

This does not mean that people will cease to say bad things about believers or the faith. That is not at all what is being communicated. However, by good words and actions they will be ashamed by the fact that their words are not founded in truth. It is a heavy burden to shoulder, as we do represent the faith to the world around us. How difficult it is to represent the Holy God of the universe to an unbelieving and perverse generation. Fortunately, the believer does not do this by his own strength or ability!

This is not simply our works and our deeds. It's not as if Christ tells the believer: "Alright, I got you saved, now get to work!" Rather, as Romans 6 and Ephesians 1–2 tell, this is to be Christ living out *His* life in the believer. The one who is born again has his life in heaven with Christ where we are eternally seated. In faithful submission and keeping His Word these works will be the natural result. Surely, Christians should examine themselves, confessing sin and living out our eternal position in our day to day lives, but we need to realize that anything that we do in our own power or strength is wasted, for only the Lord can sanctify, just as only the Lord can justify!

TITUS 2:9–10

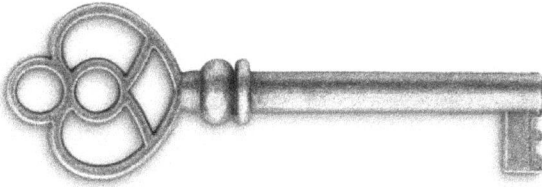

A Quick Word About Slaves

There are some important things to make mention of concerning slavery in the Roman Empire in Paul's day. First, slavery was very common, unlike today in America. However, as Americans we have a certain image of what slavery is like. There were commonalities between Roman slavery and the tragedy of slavery that befell the West in the last few centuries. Roman slaves were produced in several different ways. Someone could be born into slavery and would therefore be a slave from birth. Slaves were also taken from wars and the peoples on the borders of Roman lands. One could also be acquired as a slave from childhood, as parents were to leave a child out to be exposed. This was a wholly acceptable practice, culturally speaking. People could take those babies, raise them up and sell them as slaves. Furthermore, if a man got in a great amount of debt, he could sell himself, or a family member into slavery if he wanted.

There is a reason to draw this distinction between ancient and modern forms of slavery. Slavery was a perfectly acceptable social status. Some slaves had a lot of training and education, and we even find instances in history of slaves owning other slaves! The reason to pay close attention to this is that slavery in the Roman Empire seems to have almost more in common with our modern system of employment than the slavery that occurred in more recent American history. Though there are distinctions that cannot be ignored in our application, there is also so much similarity that it would be a poor interpretation that would disallow application into such a strikingly similar situation.

Verse 9

Urge bondslaves to be subject to their own masters in everything, to be well-pleasing, not argumentative…

Urge

This word is in italics in the translation here because it is not technically in the text. We find that the one verb is applied to the clause from the verses before ("Urge the young men..."). It is the same word that could also translated "to call alongside." However, for clarity and conciseness in English the translators chose the word "urge."

Subject

This word for "be subject to" is another word that has been examined in this study previously. It is also used in Titus 2:5. It translates the Greek word *hupotasso* and it is a compound word combining the words for "under" and "attach." This word has the meaning of attaching oneself to the underneath something in a supportive, unassuming, and uplifting way. Paul was instructing slaves not to try to rule their masters, but rather to serve them faithfully, and humbly, doing as they were told. It is of course implicit that they must disobey any order that contradicts the instruction of God.

There is a pearl of wisdom here for us today. The closest modern application point is in the workplace. A Christian should have a positive and supportive relationship to the people who are in authority over him or her. The modern concept of employment is closer to Roman citizenship than one may think. As a person relies upon having work to provide needed food and shelter that person is bound to a particular work and workplace. So then, what does the Holy Spirit tell instruct? Defensiveness? Self-promotion? Rebellion?

Godly wisdom teaches that God is most glorified when the believer lives out Christ's life by support towards those who are in authority. This attitude of submission is not conditioned upon whether the boss is likeable, or friendly. The added benefit on the material side is that a person who is supportive of the leadership is almost sure to become an asset to the company. On the spiritual side, this also provides the best example, which is most likely to generate interest in the employee's faith and motivation. Especially considering how, by the world's standards, there is an implied antagonism between a manager and his or her inferiors.

This is not to say that a Christian should be allow or invite mistreatment or abuse, nor to say that the Christian cannot offer input. It is, however, to say that if a believer can't submit to a boss or supervisor, it would be best to transfer or quit. To put it directly: "If you can't submit, you must quit!" The Christian in the workplace is not to be self-promoting and proud, but to be humble, meek, and wise.

Everything

This word is well translated "in everything" or "in all things." And that is to be the scope of the servant's obedience. We should not be constantly looking out for our own rights, or trying to protect our own reputation and pride, but rather be submissive, and supportive in all things. Once again, Biblical insight would surely tell us that to violate anything we know to go against the will of God is worth standing up about, thus in anything that the servant is asked to do that is against the will of God the servant must dissent or disobey and suffer the consequences with patience.

One's professional life should show the extent to which the believer supports authority placed over him. One should not submit one minute and then the next minute engage in gossip or backbiting, but in everything one should pay proper respect to an authority. Furthermore, a Christian is not to be self-willed or stubborn, but rather to be subject in everything.

Well-Pleasing

This is a good literal translation. This is just talking about doing the things that will please one in authority by doing things well, as we are told. If the demand is impossible or unreasonable then bringing the issue to the table in a respectful, non-offensive way is the need. This idea, as it carries over to modern work application, does not mean that believers are to be spineless, whimpering toadies. Rather strong, calm, confident, peaceful, loving Christians that are making a constant and daily choice, while displaying the wisdom and dignity that is laid out in the verses before. It is interesting that supportive employees are often labeled as "kiss-ups" or worse. This is not what Paul is saying. A good employee need not be a bootlicker. Everybody should want to have Christians working on their team because they should be the least motivated to lift themselves up, and more likely to want to serve others.

Not Argumentative

This word translates the Greek word: *antilego*. When broken up into its component parts it is *anti* (against) *lego* (speaking or talking). This is to say that there is to be no "against talking." It means that slaves were to be submissive to their masters no matter how cruel, and when the final word was laid down by the master the servant would do what the master asked.

Today it is challenging not to be argumentative. It is hard not to demand to have one's say. When a boss or manager finds something that is distasteful the first instinct is often towards self-defense. The second is to try to blame someone else. It also seems implicit in this that haggling and bickering with authorities is undesirable. Submission to correction and rebuke is desired, even if it seems unreasonable at the time.

Verse 10

*...**not pilfering**, but **showing** all **good faith** so that they will **adorn** the doctrine of **God our Savior** in every respect.*

Not Pilfering

Slaves in this day were known to be thieves. It was even a long-standing joke or a sort of stock character in Greek and Roman theater. There was always a rude or lazy servant that could be used to poke fun at the master behind his back or steal things from around the house. One Roman official even said, "Every slave we have is an enemy we harbor." This was the attitude between the two, an animosity that can be very clearly seen between bosses and employees today! Pilfering is also a huge problem amongst employees today. It is obviously inconsistent with the believer's identity in Christ, and it is always unacceptable.

Showing

This word "showing" is in the middle voice. This verb could well be translated "showing themselves" to get the idea of how emphatic and involved this action is meant to be.

Good Faith

This is meant more in the sense of being faithful and trustworthy, than the idea of showing a good faith in Christ. Christian slaves then, as Christian employees now, must be above reproach. Not every authority will be good, some may even be evil, but the mature believer is meant to be trustworthy and faithful in his or her duty. Born again souls are meant to grow into the type of person, because of Christ's constant working, whom the boss feels he or she can leave the store keys with and sleep perfectly well knowing that the business is in safe hands. This is the quality of life which Christian growth is meant to produce when the believer walks by means of the Spirit.

Adorn

We use the word "adorn" in English occasionally. It means to embellish, or to dress something up. It can mean to hang beautiful tinsel from a Christmas tree or used of a pair of earrings or a necklace on a woman. Why do we adorn things? Why do people adorn themselves? To make themselves up! To make themselves more attractive or noticeable. Good conduct, faithfulness, humility, and submission of the servant will *adorn* the doctrine (truth about, or teachings about God.)

It's amazing to think that a person can do nothing to take away from, or add to, salvation in Christ, but by actions that are simply Christ living out His life in the believer, the Bible is adorned. The Word is made more and more beautiful and amazing as it is lived out in the life of a believer.

God Our Savior

This is an interesting phrase because we find that God is called here, our Savior, which is true, however we more often see Jesus being described as the Savior. Here is further evidence from the Bible concerning the trinity. Here God the Father is given the same title as the Son: our Savior.

TITUS 2:11-12

Changing Gears

Paul has spent a few verses talking about each of the basic divisions of society in his time. He gave instructions for older men, older women, younger women, younger men and closed with slaves. Now he is changing the direction to more general information about the gospel and the way it works in the life of healthy believers. It is important to realize that this is not something that the believer is to be working to manifest in his or her life. These are character traits that will flow naturally from Christ as the center of our lives and our faith. If the believer is submitted to Christ and continually working to live out his or her eternal position in their daily condition, these are the traits and behaviors that will flow forth from union with Him.

Verse 11

*For the **grace of God** has **appeared**, bringing **salvation to all men**...*

For

This is a conjunction that denotes causality. It could be translated as "since" or "for." And in this case, it is initiating a summary statement. The Holy Spirit has been specific with different groups of people, however here there is also a general example of what godliness looks like in individual lives. These are traits and commands that apply to everyone and should be lived out in the life of every believer.

Grace of God

The grace of God has been described as God's undeserved, unearned favor toward the believer in Christ. The Greek concept of "grace" was expanded by Paul to describe all that God had done for mankind in

Christ Jesus. It was one of the great words like "love" that was given a whole new meaning and context by the Holy Spirit. In the pre-New Testament context, the Greek word simply indicated a gift, usually given to family, that could not be paid for or returned in any way shape or form. This is the wonderful gift of God through which He forgives us and purifies us of all sin.

Appeared

The Greek word here is *epiphaino* and it is where we get our English word "epiphany." It combines the word for "over, above or beyond" and the word for "appear, to shine, or to be seen." It has the idea of something that has "shined over" or "shined out!" It is also in the aorist tense, putting it in the past. This is something that has appeared before. This is pointing back to the salvation wrought by Christ on the cross.

Salvation to All Men

This is not a statement that denotes that all people are or will be saved. Quite to the opposite, the perspective of the rest of Scripture makes it clear that the sacrifice of Christ on the cross made salvation available to all men, however that does not mean that all will take God up on this offer. It is clear from Scripture that Christ's work was powerful enough to forgive all sin, and deal with every sinner (1 John 2:2; John 3:16), however His death is only appropriated to those who believe on Him. (1 John 5:1–5; John 1:12)

Verse 12

...instructing us to deny ungodliness and worldly desires and to live sensibly, righteously and godly in the present age...

Instructing

This idea of instructing is different than simply teaching. It involves discipline as well as transferring information. In the book of Proverbs and in the book of Hebrews the idea of discipline is very closely connected with the loving care of a good father. The heavenly Father also lovingly disciplines when he sees us directing our lives towards sinful and unfulfilling acts and lifestyles that God knows may be attractive in the short term, but destructive in the long run.

Deny Ungodliness

This is a negative statement. It shows that the mature believer is not merely to have godliness as a part of their lives, but also that they should stand in opposition to ungodliness. The believer doesn't simply live a godly life, but also lives in contrast to the darkness, both doing good and opposing evil. It is common to think of life in terms of weighing things out on a balance. This leads to the false idea that Christian growth is simply balancing out sinful practices with good works. Much harm has been done to the body of Christ by the unbiblical idea of penance to pay for sins. Yet, the only place that sin is paid for is at the cross of Jesus Christ. Having been finally freed from the influence and penalty of sin it only makes sense that the believer lives in opposition to that slavery from which he was made free by the work of Jesus Christ. Living in a way that is permissive or passive towards the tyranny of sin betrays a lack of understanding of the fullness of redemption that is freely given by faith in Jesus Christ.

Worldly Desires

This word "desire" can also be translated as "worldly lusts" or "worldly passions." The idea being that these are the carnal and fleshly desires that draw the believer away from God and closer to the world. This is very often equated with physical lust and sexual impurity, and this is a huge part of this word. It is especially applicable today when the assault of sexual imagery and debauchery is so commonplace. The church is surrounded by a culture that absolves such sexual sins as pornography and lust. This culture openly declares that all kinds of sexual perversion are simply natural biological impulses. So prevalent is this deception that many women have come to a point where they tolerate unfaithfulness in their husbands as if fidelity were simply impossible. The Bible states the exact opposite. Christians must not be deceived by lies of the current winds of culture. Trying to believe to be true what the Bible reveals to be false, simply because it provides an excuse to live in ungodliness, is a tragedy. This is unacceptable and the Church must deny it completely.

Sensibly

Here is our dear friend *sophronos* again. Once again conveying this idea of "wise mindedness." This is not just someone who makes wise decisions, but rather someone whose entire mindset is dominated and marked by wisdom. As we know: "The fear of the LORD is the beginning of wisdom, and the knowledge of the Holy One is understanding" (Prov 9:10). True wisdom comes from our position in Christ as His redeemed ones—positioned in His death, burial, resurrection, ascension, and seating by the will of God. This is, most often, at strict odds with worldly wisdom. Often worldly wisdom will encourage people to cut corners, or even injure others to get ahead. Godly wisdom will have none of this sort of behavior. Godly wisdom demands a heavenly perspective of the Author of Life, and His plan for the future.

Righteously

Though the teaching of Scripture is perfectly consistent regarding salvation by nothing we have done, there are still commands to a righteous life found in Scripture. Having been born again, the believer's new language is righteousness. We still suffer the influence of our sin nature that, though separated from us through our co-crucifixion with Jesus Christ, still makes demands on the believer's daily experience. We find these verses are talking about the Christian's daily condition, how life is lived out day in and day out. This is a natural outgrowth of union and growing intimacy with Jesus Christ.

Godly

This is the opposite of ungodly behavior which was warned against earlier in this verse. This suggests a reverence for God that is sometimes missing from the Church today. American evangelicals have spent quite a bit of effort to present Jesus, and thereby present God, as quiet and approachable. Having presented the idea of Jesus as a friend to the point that we don't realize that there is still a need for reverent love and respect in this relationship. There is a need to realize what it means to live in the presence of the Almighty God.

The Present Age

This present age we are in is often called the Church age. It is distinct from any other age in history and extends from Pentecost all the way to the Rapture of the Church. This is a reference to the fact that God's requirements for Church age saints differ from His requirements for Old Testament saints and differ from the way that God will interact with those saints who come to Christ during the Tribulation period. In this present age believers are freed from the law and saved completely by the grace of God by our faith in Christ, and this passage, as well as others throughout the Bible, tells how believers are to behave in this time.

TITUS 2:13

Into the Future

These verses return the focus to the Savior and his return to gather the Church, which could happen at any moment. Many churches today have been bashful to teach on the return of Christ because of the negative connotation brought by those who foolishly set dates. In an even worse turn, many churches and teachers have fallen into amillennialism and preterism, which commonly teach that Jesus will not be coming back to Earth in any physical form and totally deny a future earthly Kingdom of God that is so clearly predicted in the Bible. This is a tragic loss as Scripture teaches that Christ's eminent return is to encourage us, give us hope, and influence why we should be living Godly lives.

Verse 13

*...looking for the **blessed hope** and the **appearing of the glory** of our **great God and Savior, Christ Jesus**...*

Looking For

In Greek this is a present participle. This means that it is something that we are to be doing every day, moment by moment. The Greek word translated *looking for* here has the idea of an anticipation, a hopefulness, and a great desire to see the thing that is being sought after. Much like the anticipation of an important phone call could cause a person not to let the phone out of earshot but rather to wait and watch and hope that the call comes soon. This is the idea here. It is also important to remember the verse before: "teaching us that, denying ungodliness and worldly lusts, we should live soberly, righteously, and godly in the present age..." There is no break between those characteristics of godly living and our anxious anticipation of the coming of the Lord. Living in anticipation of the Rapture is a moral expectation in the life of a healthy believer and denying that hope is a grievous and destructive sin indeed.

The Blessed Hope

Mal Couch tells us in his commentary that this word translated "hope" can be translated "expectation, anticipation, prospect." He also tells us that it would be better translated "joyous anticipation." It is an extreme joyful longing that looks to the horizon anxiously awaiting the coming of the Lord. This is a matter of character for us. So many Christians allow Christ's return to be a sort of fairy tale in their lives, or they let it slip to the background of their thoughts until they feel that they want to cast their thoughts on it. However, this is something that should be on the forefront of the believer's thoughts constantly. This is the great promise and hope of the church. The promise that the Lord will come back to snatch his bride out of struggling, trial, and the shipwreck of this world is a directing force in a healthy Christian experience.

Appearing of the Glory

Other translations have this as "glorious appearing" however, "appearing of the glory" is closer to the Greek original. It is important to notice that this is the glory which Christ has already been given in heaven that will be displayed before all the world. It may come as a terrible shock to some, but to the believer it will be the time that is anticipated above all times. We see the doctrine of the Rapture most clearly in 1 Thessalonians 4:16–18:

> *For the Lord Himself will descend from heaven with a shout, with the voice of the archangel and with the trumpet of God, and the dead in Christ will rise first. Then we who are alive and remain will be caught up together with them in the clouds to meet the Lord in the air, and so we shall always be with the Lord. Therefore comfort one another with these words.*

Great God and Savior, Christ Jesus

This is a tricky phrase in the Greek. Those who deny the Trinity try to make it seem as if both God the Father and Jesus Christ are in view here. They are trying to teach that God, and our Savior Jesus Christ will be appearing and that is the point to which Christians look forward. The traditional interpretation, from the Church Fathers forward, is that this passage is ascribing deity to Christ.

As has been noted already in this exposition, in Roman times Caesar was considered both a god, and the savior of Rome and civilization. When Caesar went parading down the streets of a city the people were forced to cry out "Savior! Savior!" However, Paul tells the believers of his time that they have only one Savior who is Jesus Christ, and only Jesus Christ is God, not any other man. This is about Christ's appearance. In this case we must take other Scripture into account. God is never said to be appearing or coming, only Jesus. That is something that is unique to the person of Jesus Christ. This firmly establishes that Paul is trying to establish that Jesus Christ is fully God, and our only hope of salvation.

TITUS 2:14-15

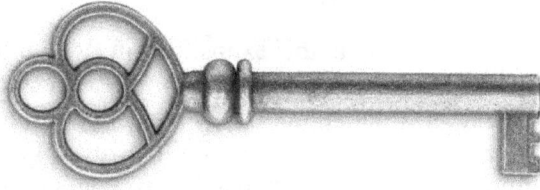

Verse 14

...who gave Himself for us to redeem us from every lawless deed, and to purify for Himself a people for His own possession, zealous for good deeds.

Who Gave Himself

This is obviously pointing back to Christ's sacrifice on the cross. Paul returns to the gospel, letting everyone know why believers can joyfully anticipate the appearance of His glory. Christians await in eager expectation of that time because of the purification by His blood, by His action and by His sacrifice alone. There is no other way that humans could have anything but fear and guilt at His next coming.

Redeem

Paul is putting the substitutionary nature of Christ's death in view here. Earlier he says that Christ gave Himself for us, and here uses the word "redeem" to describe what that "giving" achieved. This word, in Greek, means to pay a ransom, or to pay the price to free a slave or someone being held captive. It tells about how Christ's sacrifice is the one currency that could pay the debt of sin and death that was counted against sinful man. This is very serious, and a very graphic word image revealing the nature of salvation in Christ.

Every Lawless Deed

This could more succinctly be translated "all lawlessness." Paul does not make a distinction here between when those acts of lawlessness were committed, whether before or after the believer becomes saved. It is also important that he puts no limitations on this forgiveness. A human viewpoint will attach different levels to various sins thinking this one is more sinful, or worse, than that one. However, in Christ all sins are forgiven. Christ's death is sufficient for every sin, every lawless act. This is a great blessing and provides relief and assurance for all believers, as nothing can exhaust God's amazing grace.

To Purify

The most important thing to realize is who is doing the purifying. Believers who attempt to purify themselves are driven to madness trying to enact their salvation after the flesh. This, however, is neither what the Greek nor the English grammar tries to convey to us. Christ is the only one who can purify a lost sinner. Even if a person could suddenly stop sinning now and never sin again that person would still need to be purified from the sins committed previously, and from the stain of original sin from the association with Adam. It is Christ and Christ alone that purifies. When God positions a sinner in Christ Jesus, He looks and sees only the righteousness of Christ. However, when a saint is called up to Him in glory, he is freed forever from the presence of the sin nature. Praise the Lord!

For Himself

Paul explains why the Lord redeemed sinners. It wasn't exclusively his goodwill towards the helpless estate of mankind. God purified all who believe for Himself because He so much desires fellowship with mankind. He wants us to take up the places before Him bringing Him glory, honor, and praise forever and ever. The salvation which God provides to all who believe was totally voluntary on His part—He chose to be glorified through the redemption of lost mankind. Additionally, nothing that God accomplishes will fail.

People for His Own Possession

The next issue addressed is one of ownership. A common phrase says: "He is his own man!" Or, in defense of someone's individuality they will say: "I am my own person!" However, this is not what the Bible teaches. Here we see that God saved sinners, for His own glory, and for His own pleasure (Eph 1:5, 9), and such that the saints would be *His* possessions. Believers are freed, but also belong to Him who saved us. The Christian is obliged to view himself entirely as a beloved possession of the Lord. This spiritual reality, if trusted and applied, will affect the way the saint views every situation in life. Knowing that he is the property of the Lord means being able to trust that the caring hand of the Lord is at work in every situation. There can be no moment of lapse in the Lord's care for His children, but everything will now work together for good and for God's ultimate glory. This is the biblical perspective which every believer must adopt when considering the purpose of earthly existence.

Zealous for Good Deeds

Notice, it does not say "doing good deeds" or "willing to do" but "zealous for" good deeds. The natural human being has no strength to do good things that honor Christ, but it is only out of Christ's life in the believer that zeal and passion for doing good for His glory may arise!

Verse 15

***These things speak** and **exhort** and **reprove** with **all authority**. Let no one **disregard you**.*

These Things

This is a translation of the Greek word *tauta*. Here it means everything that has come before it, all the revelation that has been given to Titus by the Holy Spirit through Paul. Paul is about to charge Titus with his task. Paul sent Titus because he knew that he could get the job done, and he expected him to bring the truth to these people regardless of whose feelings were hurt, or who had to change their minds about what the faith is all about.

Speak

This word is the usual word for speak, and it is in the present tense and the imperative mood. It is a command. In English, commands usually involve leaving off the subject, i.e.: "Let the dog out!" or "Hand me that book." A command may be softened to a jussive with a simple "please" to be polite, but it is essentially a command that is being uttered. It is the same thing with these words. Paul is not suggesting that he should speak these things, but rather he is commanding him to speak these things. Furthermore, the present tense here gives the sense of immediate application. Titus is being urged to continually be speaking, even continually obeying these commands.

Exhort

This word translated "exhort" here is a word that can also be translated "council." It means that he is to speak the commands and words that Paul has told him, as well as give them wise council to apply and obey every word of it. It was not simply to fall on deaf ears, nor simply to be accepted as abstract doctrine but he was to exhort them to live by it and follow the full Word of God.

Reprove

This word "reprove" can also be translated "rebuke." It is the most extreme of the three imperatives that Titus is given. This is not just to gently steer away from bad doctrine, or to let things slide. This is a serious and strict command. In the modern world, commands to love and forgive are often more palatable, but commands from the same source to correct, reprove and rebuke appear harsh and are often unwelcome. We find here that Titus is to be ready to reprove and remove bad doctrine. He is not to tolerate bad doctrine, nor is he to make exceptions to bad doctrine because someone has some talent to offer the church. Elders are not supposed to be "professional nice guys" but strong, level-headed men of God who know the Word and are able and willing to spot bad teachings and bad theology that may impact the local church family.

All Authority

This Greek word is a powerful and forceful word. It is not something thrown around lightly but has the idea of someone giving orders as a military superior. And, as in the case of a military leader, commands and decisions are not to be questioned, nor to be refused. Surely, as a believer and as a responsible Christian leader Titus would have taught them with love and compassion, but at the same time, he was *never* to water down the message that he had to give, nor was he to compromise that message. We must remember that Titus was not preaching, or teaching, or working here under his own authority, but under God's authority. So obviously, he was not about to teach in a wishy-washy way about the truth of God!

Disregard You

"Disregard" here is translating a word that would literally be translated "think around you" or "think beyond you." It has the idea of someone who would write Titus off as not being talented enough, or old enough or something that would disqualify him from having the authority that comes only from having the Word of God as his guidance. This is essentially a warning against letting the scheming, plotting types have a foothold and destroy the church from the inside out by plotting against the spiritual leadership that has been set up by proper biblical authority.

TITUS 3:1–2

Between the Rubber and the Road

Paul continues to give instructions for godly living. It bears repeating that he is exhorting believers to live out the position that Christ has already won and freely given. He is not asking them to do these things out of their sinful flesh, but rather exhorting them to walk in the Spirit and live according to that great blessing. He is spelling out the *whys* and *hows* to what godly living looks like in daily life.

Questions immediately come to mind when issues of government are concerned. Since the time of Constantine, the image of what it is to be a Christian in society has radically changed. Before Constantine declared Christianity legal, and then later declared it the official religion of the Roman Empire, the idea of a Christian government was unimaginable. Ever since Constantine, many believers have been convinced that it is the role of the church to regulate, and affect, or even command the government. The idea of a "Christian Nation" came to the forefront of Christianity. This was the idea adopted by the Western Church, and even the reformers Calvin and Luther felt that the work of the Church was meant to establish godly governments and kingdoms here on earth.

This is very much at odds with the writings of Scripture. Rather than being commanded to overtake, or change, the government we find Paul and Peter telling Christians to be submissive to the governments where they live. This is made even more remarkable by the fact that often Christians were being persecuted and killed by the authorities!

Verse 1

Remind them to be subject to rulers, to authorities, to be obedient, to be ready for every good deed…

Remind Them

Paul tells Titus to remind everyone. This is a message for everyone, not just some, nor a few, but the whole mass of believers. This is not a selective exhortation, but a direct one. The Greek word here is *hupomimnesko*. It combines the words *hupo* meaning "under," or "cause". As well as the word *mimnesko* which is the word for "remind," or to "put into the mind of." It's not just a command to remember, but it is to cause them to remember. Paul had given this commandment before in Romans and 1 Timothy, so here Titus is to "cause them to remember."

Subject

The Greek word *hupotasso* appears again here. As in previous chapters of this book the word means, literally, to "under-attach" oneself to something else. It carries this idea of support and voluntary subjection to its object. In this case, the believer is to be subject, or "under-attached" to the government. This is fascinating that at a time when Christians were not well-treated, and coming up on a time where Christians could be killed for not worshiping the Roman Emperor as a living god. Even still, they are told to be subject. Does this mean that Paul is advocating doing things that obviously defy the will of God if the government demands it? Certainly not! Believers are only to be faithful and loyal to the demands of the government so long as the government isn't commanding disobedience to the Word and Christian conscience. However, the rest of the time believers are to submit to the laws, even the ones that we may have philosophical disagreement with (like a speed limit of 25 *mph* on a street that should clearly be limited at 40 *mph*). This is especially important because people are watching, and Paul would not have Christians viewed as anarchists.

Rulers

This word in Greek is *arche* and is where we get our English prefix "arch" as we see it in the words "arch-rival" or "archenemy." In Greek, it can simply mean the first person in a series, or the leader. Christians are to be subject to the authorities. The Holy Spirit does not seem to specifically confine this to political leaders, so it seems a fair parallel to say that the Bible commands subjection to leadership in the spheres of community, company, and government. Christians are not to be dissidents without cause, and respect for leaders is not tied to respect for them as individuals. Civil disobedience is never conditioned on merit of the fact that he or she is a scumbag, as most if not all the leaders of this time would be completely morally reprobate, and yet believers are called to "submit."

Authorities

This is not talking as much about individual leaders as the structures of authority that are set up above us. Christians are to play by the rules. The saints of God are not to be swindlers who work the system, but faithful to the authorities and the systems that are in place. The King James Version translates this as "powers," and rightly so. There are other texts which suggest that Paul is saying "be subject to rulers, who are also authorities." It matters little, seemingly, in the application as Paul is telling them that they must not malign the faith, nor the Word by their own agendas or desire to disobey the authorities. This would have been especially important in a place like Crete that was not known to be faithful to the powers that ruled it, being hugely populated with pirates, criminals, and political dissidents.

Be Obedient

It seems like this concept would be implied in the idea of submission. The inclusion of the concept of obedience shows that there is a distinction between the concepts of submission and obedience. This word has the essence of being obedient to a superior, a governor or a magistrate being particularly in view. Believers are not just to support the government and submit to it, but also to be obedient to the laws that are laid down by that authority—in so far as they do not conflict with the word of God. It would seem like a sort of double whammy, but Paul would seem to be emphasizing the Church's relationship to the governing powers.

Be Ready

This word here is to be ready, or to be prepared. Perhaps it could be likened to the idea of someone who is poised over a certain stock, or financial transaction until the time is perfect. The picture of a fisherman who waits for just the right moment to set the hook to catch the fish is also appropriate. It is a preparedness that is not lazy but watchful and diligent. It is important to notice that the Scripture here says, "ready to do every good deed" rather than simply "doing every good deed." The question that we must ask is, are we to be going out and doing good deeds indiscriminately or are we to be waiting poised for the good deeds that God has already prepared for the believer. Ephesians 2:8–10 says: *"For by grace you have been saved through faith; and that not of yourselves, it is the gift of God; not as a result of works, so that no one may boast. For we are His workmanship, created in Christ Jesus for good works, which **God prepared beforehand so that we would walk in them**."*

These well-known verses make an important point about the nature of good works in the Christian life. The good works are the result of salvation by grace through faith. Good works are not the cause of salvation, nor the evidence of salvation, they are a result of salvation and a healthy growing Christian life. These works which God prepared beforehand are not a set of actions that the Lord set up in the believer's day, but rather the character of Christ that is exhibited by grace when the believer is walking by means of the Holy Spirit. The fruit of the Spirit in Galatians 5:22–23 describes the quality of life that the Lord has prepared beforehand for the one who is growing in Christ.

Every Good Deed

This applies to the Christian as a citizen in a country, a state, a city, a county, and a community. A believer may be called upon to do something to help or assist in their community or nation. So long as the task or service isn't at odds with the revealed will of God, the task should be done cheerfully as Christians are to be the type of people that glorify God in every situation.

Verse 2

*...to **malign no one**, to be **peaceable**, **gentle**, showing every consideration for all men.*

Malign No One

This word for malign, in Greek, is the source of the English word "blaspheme." It means to speak badly against someone, or to slander their character. It brings forth another element of Christian character. The Christian is not the type of person to talk badly behind someone's back, nor the type to perpetuate rumors that are designed to hurt someone else's image or character. In other words, this is the person who does not heed silly rumors, or believable ones, and refuses to pass them on. This is especially important in terms of politics and government where someone's reputation can be everything to them. Christians ought not to be the people who are blown back and forth by the latest opinion poll, or by the latest gossip.

Peaceable

This word for peaceable here is not a positive word as it comes across in English. It is a negative word attaching the negative particle *a-* to the word for fight, or to be warlike. It is not just to be at peace but "not be fighters" or ones who are running around continually looking for a fight. This is obviously still in the context of politics and civil obedience, so it means that Christians are not to be postured with chin out and an angry glare, looking for someone to "go at it" with. The saints of God are not to be constantly trying to pick a fight with police officers or defy the authorities or get into constant arguments about politics. Believers are not to be fighters, but rather to be peaceful and gentle.

Gentle

This word could also be translated "equitable, fair, mild." It is an important quality for positive civil interaction. The Christian is not to be hot-headed and mowing over other people's views and "laying down the law" but rather fair, mild, and calm. There is no need to be a bulldozer or a powerhouse to be heard, because ultimately this government, no matter how great or bad it is, is not going to last. The only government that is going to last will be the one Jesus is coming to set up which will last for 1,000 years on this earth and then on into eternity. *That* government, *His* government, is the one to be concerned with, and there will be no wrongdoing, or need of correction there.

Every Consideration for All Men

The walk must match the talk, as the expression goes. Christian maturity is not only obedient but rather showing (the Greek could also be rendered "demonstrating") every consideration for *all* men. We are not to only respect our preferred political party, but all our leaders. We are to also show consideration for everyone who comes to our door. Showing them love and respect, even if they are those that we know to be notorious truth perverters, such as the Mormons or Jehovah's Witnesses. However, it is also important to say that, though we should show consideration for all men, it does not mean that we should have Mormons into our homes.

The fact of the matter is that opening your door to a Mormon or Jehovah's Witness can give them a foothold in the neighborhood. They can then say to the next neighbor "I just talked to Mr. Jones next door, and you know what a great Christian *he* is..." then use your well-intentioned desire to show them the truth to pervert the gospel in the minds of others. This is not, in any way, a call for us to tolerate heresy. But rather a call for us to be considerate of others. It is important to remain "wise as serpents and innocent as doves." This important truth is likewise taught in 2 John 10–11: "If anyone comes to you and does not bring this teaching, do not receive him into your house, and do not give him a greeting; for the one who gives him a greeting participates in his evil deeds."

TITUS 3:3

A Brief Look Back

Paul told Titus what he should look for in the leadership of the church and gave the picture of Christian maturity. In chapter 2, he gave specific instructions for specific groups of people. In the last two verses he talked about how Christians should behave in relation to legal and government matters. Now comes another little shift. The Holy Spirit, writing through the vehicle of Paul, here reminds believers of their natural position before they trusted Jesus Christ for salvation. The Christian must never forget his hopeless estate apart from God's saving grace. Another critical point is that the believer can take no credit for what Christ alone has done. Just when the letter may seem to emphasize works, Paul pulls back the reins and says "But remember, none of this is coming out of *your* work, *your* worthiness, or *your* power. It's all about what God has done in you, and what He is doing in terms of your daily sanctification."

Verse 3

*For **we also once** were **foolish** ourselves, **disobedient, deceived, enslaved to various lusts and pleasures, spending our life** in **malice** and **envy, hateful, hating one another**.*

We Also Once

This phrase is in the past tense. This is something that was the case before the saint trusted in Christ and was placed in Him, chronologically speaking. In the present tense the believer is to live life by trusting in the position which has been given freely by God's grace. The turning point that freed the hopeless sinner was the moment when Jesus Christ was made the object of salvation, and the free offer of life was accepted.

This should affect the believer's perspective on the unsaved. The believer is not a better person than the unbeliever, nor is the believer smarter, better, or cleverer. The reality is that the only thing that separates the believer from the unbeliever is the work of Jesus Christ. That is the primary difference. Not the lifestyle choices, not the good works, or the nice feelings, and not church attendance. Christians are set apart solely by the fact that Christ has done a good work that is applied to all who receive that gift by faith.

Foolish

This is, in the Greek, another negative word. It combines the negative particle *a-* attached as a prefix to the word for "understanding, perception or thoughtfulness." This describes someone who is thoughtless, unable to understand, and unable to perceive what would seem to be obvious to others. This is the opposite of the sensible wisdom of God.

Disobedient

Obviously, this disobedience went in all directions. Before trusting Christ, and whenever a believer chooses to walk outside of his eternal position in Christ, there is no end to disobedience. The natural man is disobedient to God, disobedient to parents, disobedient to government, and any number of other things. This disobedience comes from the flesh, also known as the sin nature. It is something that is abhorred by God and that the Christian will naturally begin to stay away from as his daily condition is conformed to the eternal position in Him.

Deceived

This is especially interesting. Foolishness is a condition. One is either wise or foolish. Disobedience depends on action or lack of action that is contrary to the authority, code, or order. The introduction of deception means that something else was acting upon the believer (and is acting still upon the non-believer) keeping their minds from being able to see things clearly. Praise the Lord for the confident anticipation of the day when: "...the devil who deceived them was thrown into the lake of fire and brimstone, where the beast and the false prophet are also; and they will be tormented day and night forever and ever" (Rev 20:10).

Enslaved to Various Lusts and Pleasures

Currently, believers may find themselves walking according to the old, fleshly ways; however, this is not consistent with the Christian's identity. Whereas once the saint was enslaved to these pleasures, lusts, and desires, he is now free to obey them, or by the power of Christ, to refuse them. The child of God is no longer under any obligation whatsoever to sin. Sin no longer owns the saint, and he is no longer obligated to obey it. Imagine a person purchased a used car and one week later finds the original owner is sitting in the driver's seat. He says, "I bought this car, and I thought I would take it out for a spin!" Obviously, the current owner would simply inform him that when he sold the car, he no longer had any right to take it for a spin. He can only ever drive the car with the current owner's permission. It is the same now with the Christian life. Sin does not own the believer any longer. God is the permanent owner.

Spending Our Life

The concept contained here is how one leads their life. When in unbelief, a person can only lead their life according to the terrible tyranny of these sinful traits. An unbeliever may seem like a good person according to human standards and perspectives; however, they are involuntarily caught in a web much deeper than they can escape on their own. They may spend their whole lives trying to saw out of the net in which they are caught; and, for all their good deeds, not break a single strand of the cords that make up the snare.

Malice

This word, in Greek, is from the root word that simply means evil. This describes the sort of evil that delights in the pain and injury of others. This is the kind of evil that cheers when the good guy is hurt, and the kind of evil that would throw a parade for the turncoat. This word is not the sort of word that is thrown around lightly and used jokingly, but rather a horrible truth about the true nature of man. Man is by nature corrupt, evil, and dark spirited. The sin nature celebrates in the destruction of others. That sin nature that is so offended by all light and good in the world.

Envy

Envy is all too familiar to the human experience. Envy, or jealousy, can be one of the most destructive forces in human relationships. Jealousy can destroy a marriage so quickly it can seem like it was never there to begin with. Few sinful emotions can have such a quick and ravaging effect on any given relationship. It can be so subtle:

"You are so lucky. I wish I had that advantage..."

"Why were you looking at him?"

*"I wish I could have that car. I deserve it more than **he** does!"*

Envy builds up so many walls and destroys so many relationships that it would be impossible to count the examples even in our own lives.

Hateful

This does not mean filled with hate, but rather something that is so characterized by hate that we find that there is no other response to it but hatred. Other words that would translate this Greek word may be "despicable" or "detested." It brings new meaning, knowing that this was the natural standing of sinful man before salvation in Christ brings transformation. According to Romans 5:8: "But God demonstrates His own love toward us, in that while we were yet sinners, Christ died for us."

Hating One Another

The Greek has the idea of us *continually* hating one another. Outside of Christ there is nothing but shades of hatred and distrust. Not only is the natural man hateful and detestable, but he also hates everyone else because everyone else is just a mirror of what hateful creatures humans are apart from the Lord Jesus Christ. This picture of all that humanity is apart from Christ, like *The Picture of Dorian Gray*, should cause all to shudder with fear and fill grateful eyes with holy tears praising God for the work that He has done on behalf of hopeless sinners. The believer ought never cast a judgmental eye on the non-believer because of the constant reminder that "but for the grace of God, there go I."

TITUS 3:4–5

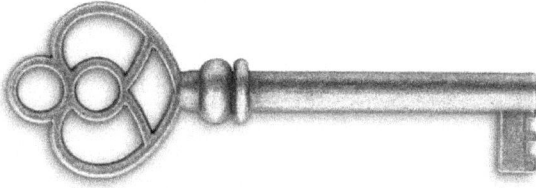

Where We've Been

Keeping the context is one of the most important rules of Biblical interpretation. When verses are allowed to be taken out of context all manner of erroneous interpretations can result. This demands an attitude mindful of what has come before and after the passage in view. Verse three described the position of humanity apart from Christ. The picture was painted of hopeless sinners, enslaved to lust, disobedience, and foolishness. This is the current condition of every person who is not in Christ. The discussion continued to describe how believers can continue to walk in the foolish and wretched ways that enslaved them before salvation. However, Paul is about to share the good news!

Verse 4

*But when the kindness of **God our Savior** and His **love for mankind** appeared…*

But

With this conjunction Paul is drawing a distinction. Verse three illustrated a person's position apart from Christ, and then he goes on to draw the distinct picture of what has happened to the believer, and what is happening currently as the believer grows in Christ. He even takes this opportunity to make sure that the gospel of grace is clearly illustrated. The Holy Spirit portrays that the unbeliever is weak and unable to help himself. The believer is still weak and unable to help himself in his own power. Everything depends on total reliance upon Christ!

God Our Savior

This unique phrase appears again. The emperor worship would be especially prominent in Crete given the rocky history of the island of

Crete and becoming a part of the Roman Empire. This is one of the many issues in Roman culture that gave the Christians a lot of trouble!

The other thing this alerts us to is the fact that God and Jesus seem to be interchangeably referred to as "our Savior." It is, by equivalence, a testament to the deity of Christ. It is also important to know that the definite article is present before the word Savior. Meaning that it is specific: *"The Savior* of us." He is not "one of the ones who saved us," nor is he "like a savior." He is the one and only Savior of all who believe.

Love for Mankind

This word, in Greek, is where we get our English word Philanthropy. It is a compound word involving the two words *phileo* meaning "brotherly love" and the word *anthropos* meaning man, or mankind. It is literally: loving of all mankind. This verse is a stick in the spokes of those who would be proponents of limited atonement (the idea that Jesus only died for the elect and His sacrifice is only sufficient for those who are chosen). Rather this verse tells us that God's love in sending Christ to die on the cross was one that extended to every person even if they would reject His plans to redeem them.

Appeared

This word is where we get our English *epiphany*. It has the idea of being revealed or appearing. This word means that the love of God for mankind has shone forth from Calvary. No one, knowing the truth, can paint a picture of a God who is hateful or who loves to torture His creation. His love has shone through all the lies and misconceptions that this world may have about our Lord.

Verse 5

*He saved us, **not on the basis of deeds** which we have done in righteousness, **but according to His mercy,** by the **washing of regeneration** and **renewing** by **the Holy Spirit**...*

He Saved Us

Let's do some basic grammar here: What is the subject of the sentence? *He.* What is the verb? *Saved.* What is the object? *Us.* We didn't save ourselves, nor are we responsible for any part of it. He saves us. There is no exception. Another important point about this verb is that it is an effective aorist. This could be most simply interpreted as meaning that it is something that is finished, done in the past. It doesn't ever need to be redone and it will not be undone. This is a secure and finished process. He saved us.

Not on the Basis of Deeds

So here we see one of the most important teachings in all of Scripture. This flies in the face of every man-centered, work- based, system of theology ever invented. Whether Catholics, Mormons, Jehovah's Witnesses or Muslims, it is the same thing every time: People working to be saved. The Bible is clear: That is impossible! Jesus did not save on the basis of good works, nor did He start salvation and look to humanity to finish the work. It is complete and total. There is nothing that a human can do to counterbalance the stain and weight of sin. Even if someone could manage to spend the rest of their life doing good things and, in the end, had done better than most, they would find that their very nature is "hateful and hating one another" and worthy of nothing but destruction!

But According to His Mercy

This "but" is different from the one before. The last "but" (in verse 4) was a conjunction that denoted a change in direction in the argument. This Greek word translated "but" is a strong contrastive "but". We find that this is a black and white thing. Salvation is not at all by works but rather it is according to the Lord's great mercy. This mercy is the type that is shown unto the pitifully helpless. Realize that there was *no* thing that we could do for ourselves. True poverty is a wretched condition indeed. There is no way for them to escape their poverty no matter how much they want to, or how hard they try, the money is just not there to be earned. It is a total and complete helplessness that points all hope to the Lord and to His great mercy.

Washing

This word "washing" is a word that means washing something for sacrificial use, or even to be used in the temple in Jerusalem. This is the word that was used for things being washed and dedicated to holiness. This is the way in which Christ has washed the believer.

Of Regeneration

This word "regeneration" is a good fit to the Greek. Combining the prefix "re-", meaning "again," and "generation" implying "birth." This is a reference to the rebirth that comes from believing in Jesus. The believer is born again. Two obvious references that come to mind when considering this idea of "new birth" are John 3:3: "Jesus answered and said to him, 'Truly, truly, I say to you, unless one is born again, he cannot see the kingdom of God.'" As well as 2 Corinthians 5:17: "Therefore if anyone is in Christ, he is a new creature; the old things passed away; behold, new things have come."

Renewing

We see time and time again that the word "new" or "renewed" as applied to the believer is not talking about new in time (as in something that is just freshly made, or as a used car can be "new to you" even though it's been around for a couple of years). This word for "new" is something that is new in kind, or something that had never been seen before. It is this life that is given to the Christian and the new quality of creature that he has become. The world had never seen anything like what the Lord has done in the life of the believer; it cannot be copied, or even approximated by the world.

The Holy Spirit

And who is the great agent of this great action? The Holy Spirit! All three members of the Trinity are intimately involved in our salvation. What an amazing blessing it is to know that the whole Godhead works together perfectly to provide salvation. It is not as if one of the members of the Trinity split the vote and majority rules. The persons of the triune God are all in agreement and all willing to go well beyond the end of human imagination to save us each and individually! Praise the Lord!

TITUS 3:6–7

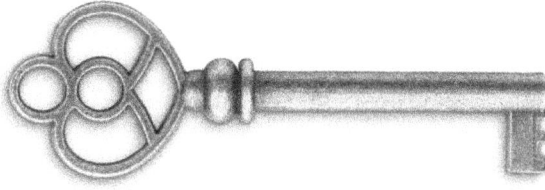

Verse 6

*...whom He **poured** out upon us **richly through Jesus Christ our Savior**...*

Whom

Whom indeed? There are two questions that need to be answered. The first is: Who is Paul talking about? The verse immediately before tells quite clearly that the pronoun "He" refers to the Holy Spirit. Yet there is another easily missed point. The Holy Spirit is not a thing but rather a person. He is a personality not an impersonal, unknowable force like the new age teachers may teach, or even as Islam teaches. The Holy Spirit is a knowable personality, not a blind force that cannot be seen, heard, or known.

Poured

This is a cool word in Greek, and the English translation "poured" does not quite catch the whole meaning of it. In English, the word "poured" can suggest something with a spout that can carefully and precisely pour just the right amount without spilling a drop. This word may very often recall a pitcher pouring water. This word, however, is much bigger than that! It could also be translated "spilled" or even "sloshed." The idea is that the Father doesn't just carefully pour the right amount of "the Holy Spirit" into our lives as if He wanted to save some for later. He generously throws Himself into believers with His grace and power, like a child joyously throwing a bucket full of water on his friend during a hot summer's water fight.

Richly

Next comes the idea of riches related to the Holy Spirit. The book of Ephesians is littered with references to "the riches of His grace" and the book of Philippians tells us about how the Lord will meet the Christian's need according to His "glorious riches in Christ Jesus." The references go on and on, but what is being communicated is that we are rich because of what God has given in the Spirit. Furthermore, He poured it out richly! It is amazing that God doesn't give us "just as much as we can handle" and He doesn't give in a way that is cheap or begrudging. Furthermore, there is no "Holy Spirit *lite*" or "*Diet* Holy Ghost" that is offered. God richly gives of His riches in Christ and fills the believer with His Holy Spirit. There are no take backs and no half portions! We don't need to beg Him for more of His Holy Spirit, nor do we need to go in for a "refill" every week. He is constantly, richly pouring Himself out upon everyone who has believed!

Through

This word through is "*dia*" in the Greek and has the idea of agency. It gives us the picture that Jesus is the instrument through which the Father gives the gift of the Holy Spirit.

Jesus Christ Our Savior

This is a special verse for a couple of reasons. Firstly, we see here that Paul is giving Jesus the title of "Savior" once again. This could be most literally translated: "The Savior of us." This is the same thing that was said earlier about God the Father (Tit 1:3). So, quite obviously, by equivalence the deity of God the Son is once again shown to be the orthodox Biblical teaching. There is no doubt about the fact that all the New Testament authors held firmly to the absolute Godship of the Son, Jesus Christ.

The second thing that is special about this verse is that it shows all three members of the Trinity working perfectly together in their divinity and their different parts in our salvation. Here we see very clearly God the Father pouring God the Holy Spirit into our lives by means of God the Son. This is yet more clear Biblical evidence of the doctrine of the trinity.

Verse 7

*...so that **being justified** by His **grace** we **would be** made heirs **according to** the **hope** of eternal life.*

Being Justified

This is the only place in the pastoral epistles that Paul writes about the justification that the believer has in Christ. This word justification has a legal definition. In a court of law, it was the duty of the judge to declare a person guilty or innocent. It is in this way that Christians are justified. God views believers as having the righteousness that Christ had and views the penalty as being paid by Christ's perfect work on the cross. Notice a few things:

1. This is a completed past action. Believers are not being justified (like a process) we *are justified.*

2. This is, in Greek as well as English, in the passive voice. The believer does not justify himself but is justified.

3. Think about the court illustration. If a prisoner is brought to trial and is completely justified before the court that justification stands. He need not worry about being tried again on the same terms. This justification is God's holy and righteous judgment, and nothing is going to change it.

Grace

Once again, we see this doctrine of grace appear. It is the inescapable fact of Scripture. Christians are saved by God's grace, sanctified by His grace, and glorified by His grace. Furthermore, Ephesians 2:7 makes it clear that we will spend all of eternity watching the glory of His grace be revealed to us. We will spend eternity in awe of this great grace that is one of God's most amazing characteristics.

Would Be

This is a difficult passage to translate. The subjunctives give the sense that something may or may not happen, or that it is somehow dependent upon the believer to get the ball rolling. In this case it could even give the idea that His grace came that Christians could be heirs, but also may miss that entirely. This meaning, however, is not found in the Greek. In the Greek it is quite clear that it is something that has already been given and received. We are already heirs, and it is God's grace that has done that great work in the believer!

According To

This word "according to" here is *kata* and it means "in full accordance with" meaning that this is something that is in keeping with another promise that we have in Christ which is the promise of eternal life. These two things are entirely in keeping with each other. It is God's great pleasure to save us, as well as to sanctify us, so that he can demonstrate His glory all throughout eternity.

Hope

The word "hope" in English is not the same as its Greek translation. It must be understood that "hope", in the Biblical sense, is something that is a sure thing. The saints of God are not to walk around thinking: "I hope I have eternal life." Rather, assurance of salvation is the birthright of the Christian. The child of God can view every struggle and trial with the knowledge of the fact that he or she has been made an heir and permanently given the gift of eternal life! Hallelujah!

TITUS 3:8

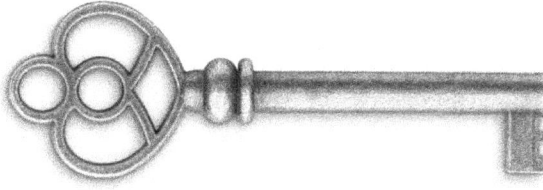

Verse 8

*This is a **trustworthy statement**; and **concerning** these things I **want** you to **speak confidently**, so that those who have **believed** God will be **careful** to **engage in good deeds**. These things are **good and profitable** for men.*

Trustworthy Statement

Trustworthy here translates the Greek word *pistos* which is more commonly translated as "faith" or "faithful." This is the same basic word from Titus 1:6 claiming that an elder should have faithful children. Even more interestingly, it is identical to Titus 1:9 where elders are commanded to be "holding fast the faithful word." Paul is saying that this is, just as the rest of Scripture, good doctrine that is worthy to be taught, learned, and applied. What, however, is it that is a "trustworthy statement"? Titus 3:5–7:

He saved us, not on the basis of deeds which we have done in righteousness, but according to His mercy, by the washing of regeneration and renewing by the Holy Spirit, whom He poured out upon us richly through Jesus Christ our Savior, so that being justified by His grace we would be made heirs according to the hope of eternal life.

Paul is affirming the statement he made before, which is one of the clearest statements of the gospel, and what takes place in the life of the believer at the moment of belief. This is what he calls "faithful word" to which he earlier told the elders to hold fast! The fact that he would use these words so closely together is a good argument that Paul knew beyond a shadow of a doubt that he was writing Scripture.

Concerning

This is the word *peri* which can be translated "around" or "concerning." It can mean in a physical sense to go around something, but here it very obviously takes on the contextual meaning of concerning or regarding this. This verse concerns the profession of the gospel. In these verses Paul is quite clear about the believer's position. There is no law to be fulfilled, nor is there any good thing to do to gain salvation. This contradicts the worldly false doctrine: "bad people go to hell; good people go to heaven." It is not by good works that we are saved, and we are supposed to speak out concerning this issue.

Want

Boulomai is the Greek word here. It has the sense of something that is desired, or even yearned for. Vine's notes[7] that it is one of the stronger words for desire. This is not something that Paul wants casually, but it is a serious and deep desire that they would be involved in this assertion of the gospel. It is also quite personal. Paul deeply desires that Titus would boldly preach the gospel. Surely the desire for all to spread the gospel is implicit in this command. The importance of spreading the gospel of Christ cannot be a command limited to the first century!

Speak Confidently

Other translations have this as "assert strongly." Paul's wish is that the gospel would be professed boldly and consistently. This one Greek word contains the meaning that Paul wanted the Word preached both boldly and seriously, especially around the issue of the gospel. This should be the most confident declaration of the Christian. Modern American culture has declared it a faux pas to even mention issues of faith in daily discussion, yet believers are not required to fulfill the demands of the culture. The Christian is not of this world any longer and needs not play by its rules when it comes to sharing the good news about the Lord Jesus Christ.

---

[7] W. E. Vine and Merrill Unger, *Vine's Complete Expository Dictionary of Old and New Testament Words* (Nashville, TN: Thomas Nelson, 1996).

Believed

Here the word "believed" is in the perfect tense and the active voice. There is great significance to each of these things. Firstly, the perfect tense indicates that the belief was a completed past action that has ongoing effects into the present. It is not conditioned upon anything else, simply belief. The active voice displays the fact that the believer is actively choosing to believe. The Holy Spirit is not believing for the believer, but rather a person will decide to believe God and His gospel, or not, and God's judgment will be made on that crux of that issue.

Careful

This word could be literally translated "mindful" or to be "seriously in consideration of the thing." It means to concentrate on doing something. This is not just: "that they would do..." but rather: "that they would do deliberately, with careful consideration."

Engage In Good Deeds

What's this? After all the time spent in this letter, in Romans, and in countless other passages talking about how salvation is by faith through grace, now Paul is going back to this good works thing? How can that be? What can possibly be going on here? It is of the utmost importance to realize that Paul is not saying "...and if they don't do this, they are going to lose their salvation!" Quite to the contrary, that would mean that our salvation was based on something other than faith, that is, our continuing good deeds!

Paul agrees with James here. Just like the James 2 passages, this is often misapplied as a passage that suggests that salvation can be lost. "Thus, also faith by itself, if it does not have works, is dead. But someone will say, 'you have faith, and I have works.' Show me your faith without your works, and I will show you my faith by works" (Jas 2:17–18). Good works are to be the outflow of faith in Christ. If we believe this gospel is true and that while we could do nothing for ourselves God saved us (Rom 5:8) the natural outflow of that is to submit ourselves to God and, walking by the empowerment of the Holy Spirit, walk in the good works God has set aside for us to do (Eph 2:9–10).

Good and Profitable

Here is a restatement and an addition. The acting out of good works based on our position in Christ is good! It is good for the doer of these good works as by submission of our members to the Holy Spirit we are sanctified (Rom 6:13). But it is also good and profitable for the recipient of those good works. If it is a believer, the believer will obviously be encouraged in love and in faith having beheld the mighty working of Christ's life through another believer. If the recipient is a non-believer, he or she will certainly have beheld something of what the life of Christ and the gospel is all about. This may be the tool that the Lord uses to bring them to Himself! Careful, thoughtful, good works that proceed forth from reliance upon Christ are good and profitable to all men. Though we are not earning, proving, or preserving our salvation by those good works, we are acting out of the great gift of salvation that has been given us.

You can inspire loyalty by being able to take someone's house, but the greatest loyalty will come if the house is freely given.

TITUS 3:9–11

Last Orders

Paul will get one last jab in for the believers to continue in the grace that God has given which will result in living godly lives and doing good deeds. This is the last doctrinal instruction given to Titus in this book. It is here that Paul finishes off this beautiful letter without which the church would be massively impoverished in information of God's design for His Church. These last few commands are incredibly important for preserving the unity of the faith. There is more to this than it would appear, and things are not always cut and dried, nor are they always easy. This is a challenge for the believer and a challenge to the Church to live up to the high task that God has given it!

Verse 9

*But **avoid foolish controversies** and **genealogies** and strife and **disputes about the Law**, for they are **unprofitable and worthless**.*

Avoid

The word is a clear command to stay away from something. In the Greek it is in the present tense, the middle voice, and the imperative mood. The present tense has the sense of current action. The middle voice is unique to the Greek language. It is extreme involvement of the subject in the action. Often, it indicates reflexive action, or that the subject is to be especially involved in the execution of that action. In this case it seems to be reflexive. So what Paul is writing would be equivalent to the extended translation: "You specifically, right now, be keeping yourself from foolish controversies..." It is a very intense and specific command that Titus needs to be living out by the Spirit's empowerment day-by-day, just as we do.

Foolish Controversies

The Greek word that is here translated "foolish" is the source of the English word "moron." So, it's not just something that's silly, it's moronic or stupid to engage in this kind of talk and argument. The word translated "controversies" is translated as "questions" in the KJV. So, believers are not to spend time rolling over stupid controversies in discussion and debate. Mature believers are not to fight over these things! Biblical unity and love for one another should be much stronger than this! There is a point where two believers can sharpen one another "as iron sharpens iron" (Prov. 27:17), and there is another point altogether where the discussion devolves to people talking to hear their own voice. Examples of this kind of prattle would be "How many angels can dance on the head of a pin?" or "Would Jesus be a Republican or a Democrat?" These endless debates produce no godliness and reflect poorly on the Church.

Genealogies

This is something with a distinctly Jewish flavor and application. Jesus had a human linage; these are clearly laid out in the gospels of Luke and Matthew. Until AD 70, when the Temple was destroyed, one could go to the temple and check the work of Matthew and Luke. The fact that no one disputed those claims in the early years is a large testament to the accuracy of those genealogies. However, the Jews of this time would claim to have authority based on their closeness to Christ in their ancestry, and Paul is clear that this is also to be avoided.

Disputes about the Law

This is also a Jewish issue. The Jews would have endless squabbles about how far one could go before it was a sin. How far a person could walk from their house on the Sabbath, or whether it was lawful to eat an egg that was laid on the Sabbath (because that chicken really shouldn't have been working on the Sabbath!). And on and on! Paul is clear that these nit-picky points of the law are no longer profitable for the believer because we are no longer under law as Galatians and Romans so clearly conclude.

Unprofitable and Worthless

The reasons for this are two. One is that they are without profit for the believer. The Christian does not gain anything from the use of these controversies and disputes about the Law. It is unprofitable because the Law is death to the believer! But it is not just without any benefit, it is also without use! This is not mere redundancy. The believer cannot benefit from these sorts of controversies, nor can he use them to further behold the Lord Jesus, nor to pursue the victorious Christian's life that the Lord would have us live!

Verses 10–11

*Reject a **factious man** after a first and second warning, knowing that such a man is **perverted and is sinning**, being **self-condemned**.*

Reject

The word translated "reject" is a compound word that has a lot of force. It has the sense of "throwing to the side." There is a distinct idea of getting this person out of the way of the body. The people who are in our church bodies trying to make cliques and clubs, especially surrounding wrong or imbalanced teaching, need to be rejected after two warnings. This is, in the Greek, an imperative. This is not merely a suggestion!

Factious Man

The word translated "factious" is where we get our English word "heretic." It is a divisive person who is specifically teaching bad or unbalanced doctrine. This is a person who, after being warned twice, will not reform his teaching. Sometimes these teachers are very clearly trying to accrue a following for themselves. At other times they may just be propounding a false doctrine. In either case if they refuse to change their ways after two warnings they must be put aside.

Perverted and Sinning

People who are teaching blatantly anti-Biblical doctrines or who are argumentative regarding their bad doctrine rather than desiring to come to a clear understanding of what the Bible says, are covering up some serious sin in their lives. False doctrine is used to cover up some secret sin that the believer desires to continue. In this respect, putting them out of the church is a merciful act because it isolates them and leaves them alone with their sins. When forced to evaluate it alone the Holy Spirit may have a better chance to convict them of their foolishness. This word for "perverted" literally means "turned inside-out." They are completely backwards and cannot be helped in the church any longer.

Self-Condemned

The Greek here is clear, this person knew the consequences and took it upon themselves. This is the most merciful thing that can be done by the church, and God's prescribed way to break through—the false teachers must be expelled.

TITUS 3:12–15

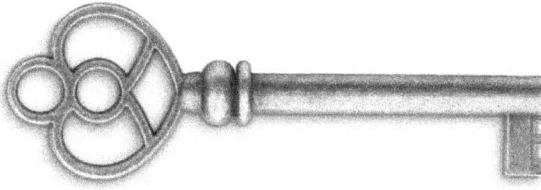

Verse 12

*When I send **Artemas or Tychicus** to you, **make every effort to come to me at Nicopolis**, for I have decided to spend the winter there.*

Artemas or Tychicus

Titus was laying the groundwork for others to come in and continue what he began. Tychicus is mentioned as a faithful helper and assistant to Paul (Acts 20:4; Eph 6:21; Col 4:7; and 2 Tim 4:2). The point is that both men were faithful servants of the gospel and of the Church. One or the other was being sent to Crete so that Titus could move on and head to Nicopolis.

Make Every Effort to Come to Me at Nicopolis

Here we see that someone else is being sent to take Titus' place so that he can meet Paul at Nicopolis. Some commentators think that Paul could feel the end finally closing in and wanted to arrange to be with Titus one last time. The benefits to meeting in Nicopolis would have been manifold. Firstly, it was a good compromise so neither of them had to traverse the entire distance between them. Secondly, it was reputed to be a bit less cold and forbidding in the winter.

Verse 13

***Diligently help** Zenas **the lawyer** and Apollos on their way so that **nothing is lacking for them**.*

Diligently Help...Nothing Is Lacking for Them.

Here we see that Zenas and Apollos are being sent. This isn't just a pleasure trip, but the word translated "on their way" has the idea of a journey that one has been sent on, rather than something simply done of their own initiative, for personal or business reasons. This verse is an example of Paul commanding the need for physical support of missionaries, teachers, or ministers. We find here that Paul is telling Titus that he should make sure that their needs are met as they continue their way. Titus would, presumably, draw this support from the churches on the Island of Crete.

The Lawyer

This word is the word *nomikos* and is based on the word for "law." It is not a sure thing, but it is probably best translated as "lawyer." This proves, contrary to all our instinctual understanding, that lawyers really can be saved! Hallelujah!

Verse 14

Our people *must also learn to engage in good deeds to meet pressing needs,* ***so that they will not be unfruitful.***

Our People

This seems to refer to the Christians who are in Crete. Even in closing the letter Paul is driving home the point of how believers should behave towards others. This would seem to be an exhortation that the believers are to support ministry, missionaries, and other believers!

So That They Will Not Be Unfruitful

It even seems shocking now, but Paul seems to equate this provision for these ministries with their fruitfulness. It shows us that giving, hospitality and provision for others is a vital part of the Christian life. It is something that is called "fruitful." This is one way we can gauge our heart before the Lord. If we are giving freely from what we have that is one sign that we are in a good place. If we are unable to give freely from the good things that the Lord has provided, we may find ourselves not surrendered to the Lord in other areas of life as well.

Verse 15

All who are with me greet you. Greet those who love us in [the] faith. **Grace be with you all.**

Grace Be with You All

So, Paul closes with the warmth that has characterized the entire letter. He sends greetings from all who are with him, many of whom Titus may have known his entire Christian life. He also sends Paul's greetings to all those "who love us in faith." It seems Paul couldn't end this masterpiece of divinely inspired writing without emphasizing one last time what it is that characterizes our existence as believers. There is no escaping the fact that God's grace is the only thing that has brought us this far, and as the hymn says, "grace will lead me home."

SCRIPTURE INDEX